Unequal Choices

The American Campus

Founded by Harold S. Wechsler

The books in the American Campus series explore recent developments and public policy issues in higher education in the United States. Topics of interest include access to college, and college affordability; college retention, tenure and academic freedom; campus labor; the expansion and evolution of administrative posts and salaries; the crisis in the humanities and the arts; the corporate university and for-profit colleges; online education; controversy in sport programs; and gender, ethnic, racial, religious, and class dynamics and diversity. Books feature scholarship from a variety of disciplines in the humanities and social sciences.

For a list of all the titles in the series, please see the last page of the book.

Unequal Choices

· ·

How Social Class Shapes Where
High-Achieving Students Apply
to College

YANG VA LOR

Rutgers University Press
New Brunswick, Camden, and Newark, New Jersey
London and Oxford, UK

Rutgers University Press is a department of Rutgers, The State University of New Jersey, one of the leading public research universities in the nation. By publishing worldwide, it furthers the University's mission of dedication to excellence in teaching, scholarship, research, and clinical care.

Library of Congress Cataloging-in-Publication Data
Names: Va Lor, Yang, author.
Title: Unequal choices : how social class shapes where high-achieving students apply to college / Yang Va Lor.
Description: New Brunswick, New Jersey : Rutgers University Press, [2023] | Series: The American campus | Includes bibliographical references and index.
Identifiers: LCCN 2022030056 | ISBN 9781978827059 (hardback) | ISBN 9781978827042 (paperback) | ISBN 9781978827066 (epub) | ISBN 9781978827080 (pdf)
Subjects: LCSH: Children with social disabilities—Education. | Educational equalization. | College choice. | Universities and colleges—Admission—Social aspects.
Classification: LCC LC4065 .V33 2023 | DDC 378.1/61—dc23/eng/20220902
LC record available at https://lccn.loc.gov/2022030056

A British Cataloging-in-Publication record for this book is available from the British Library.

References to internet websites (URLs) were accurate at the time of writing. Neither the author nor Rutgers University Press is responsible for URLs that may have expired or changed since the manuscript was prepared.

♾ The paper used in this publication meets the requirements of the American National Standard for Information Sciences—Permanence of Paper for Printed Library Materials, ANSI Z39.48-1992.

rutgersuniversitypress.org

Manufactured in the United States of America

Contents

Unequal Choices

Introduction

• •

Jack and Lan are two high school seniors from the San Francisco Bay Area. They are both considered high-achieving students, with GPAs of at least an A– and SAT or ACT scores that put them among the top 10 percent of all test takers (Hoxby and Avery 2012). Jack has a 4.05 GPA, scored a 34 out of 36 on the ACT, and he has a combined SAT Math and Reading score of 1370 out of 1600. Jack lives with his mother, who did not attend college and who works as an in-home care provider. Lan, on the other hand, is the son of an editor for a nonprofit organization and an accountant. Lan has a 4.36 GPA and a combined SAT Math and Reading score of 1440. Because of Jack and Lan's stellar academic records, there is a general expectation that these two highly qualified students will apply to the nation's leading colleges and universities.

Despite having similar levels of academic achievement, the college application choices of these two students are quite different. Lan, the middle-class student, did what was expected. He submitted applications to leading universities across the country: four Universities of California (UCs), multiple Ivy League universities, and several top liberal arts colleges in the Midwest and on the East Coast. Jack, the working-class student, on the other hand, limited his college choices to those close to home in California. He applied to multiple California State Universities (CSUs), some UCs, and an in-state private university.

Why are the college choices of these two students so different despite the fact that they have similar academic records? If we delve deeper into their backgrounds and experiences, it becomes clear that their decisions are driven by considerations beyond just their academic ability. Instead, the college choices of these two students are largely shaped by their upbringing, experiences, and expectations. Lan, for example, came from a household in which both of his parents completed college. He attended one of the top public schools in the region; students at his school have successfully applied to colleges across the country and even abroad. Moreover, he has traveled throughout the United States and other parts of the world with student clubs or while accompanying his father on his work trips. Lan's decision about where to submit college applications was driven largely by academic fit, institutional prestige, and the desire to accumulate new experiences in a different part of the country.

Whereas Lan's decision largely reflected the fulfillment of his personal desires, Jack's decision was driven by family considerations and geographic limitations. While Jack grew up in a city infamous for a struggling educational system, he was able to enroll in what was considered one of the top public schools in his district. The school enrolled students from across the city, and it was well known for its academic programs and the economic diversity of its student body. Though most students at his high school applied to colleges in California, Jack was aware that some students have attended top colleges beyond the state. When it came to his college decisions, however, concern for the health and well-being of his mother significantly influenced his decision. As the only child, he has had to support his mother to navigate life in the city. He remarked, "For her, I have to make a lot of decisions, which I don't feel like making." He wanted to apply only to colleges where he could drive home at a moment's notice in case of a family emergency. He satisfied this consideration by limiting his choices to colleges within California.

The college application choices of Lan and Jack are not unique. They reflect the patterns underlying how students from different family backgrounds make decisions about where to apply to college. Research consistently points to the significance of social class background in shaping which colleges highly qualified high school students apply to and where they attend college. High-achieving students from socioeconomically disadvantaged backgrounds are more likely to end up at less selective institutions compared to their socioeconomically advantaged peers with similar academic qualifications (Karabel and Astin 1975; Hill and Winston 2006; McPherson and Schapiro 2006; Lopez Turley, Santos, and Ceja 2007; Hoxby and Avery 2012).

In *Unequal Choices*, I examine the college application choices of high-achieving students, looking closely at how their decisions are influenced by the larger contexts of family, school, and community. I show that social class differences in where students submit college applications are shaped not only by access to information but by the context in which such information is received and the life experiences that students draw upon to make sense of higher education. For students today, institutional contexts, such as high schools and college preparation programs, shape the type of colleges that students deem appropriate, while family upbringing and personal experiences influence how far from home students imagine they can apply to college. Additionally,

I identify several mechanisms in the reproduction of social inequality, showing how institutions and families of the middle and upper-middle class work to procure advantages by cultivating dispositions among their children for specific types of higher education opportunities.

The Structure of Higher Education

To put the college choices of the students discussed in this book into perspective, it is important to provide some background information on the historical transformation and current structure of the higher education system in the United States. In other words, what are the different college options? And what are the consequences of pursuing certain types of colleges over others? Since the 1940s, the system of higher education in the United States has undergone tremendous expansion, prompted largely by the post–World War II economic boom and, in particular, by provisions in the G.I. Bill that subsidized higher education (Bowles and Gintis 1976; Roska et al. 2007). Over the past several decades, access to postsecondary education has improved for all segments of society, especially those from disadvantaged groups. However, given the fact that most of the expansion of higher education occurred at the level of community colleges or two-year colleges, unequal access to different types of colleges and universities remains (Ayalon et al. 2008). The stratification of higher education as evidenced by the emergence of an educational hierarchy with elite education at the top and mass education below has constrained student opportunities. As Josipa Roska and her colleagues (2007) described, "The mass sector developed a diversified range of lower-status academic institutions and vocationally oriented programs, while the elite institutions maintained academic focus and selectivity, resulting in a highly stratified system of U.S. postsecondary education" (168).

Given the structure of higher education in the United States, upon graduation from high school, students are faced with a myriad of postsecondary educational options. They can choose among vocational schools, two-year colleges, or four-year colleges. Among four-year colleges, students can choose to attend a public or private institution and one with more or less prestige. One of the key indicators of institutional prestige is selectivity. Selectivity is a measure of the academic profiles of admitted students, specifically student scores on the SAT I and ACT aptitude tests.

While there are a number of different ways to distinguish among colleges on the basis of selectivity, the most referenced studies on college selectivity typically utilize the selectivity classification in *Barron's Profiles of American Colleges*. Researchers Caroline Hoxby and Christopher Avery (2012) used selective colleges to "refer to colleges and universities that are in the categories from 'Very competitive plus' to 'most competitive' in *Barron's Profiles of American Colleges*.

There were 236 such colleges in the 2008 edition. Together, these colleges have enrollments equal to 2.38 times the number of students who scored at or above the 90th percentile on the ACT and SAT 1" (5).

Examples of selective colleges within the state of California include institutions such as Stanford University, the University of Southern California, and all the University of California campuses with the exception of UC Riverside and UC Merced. Among the CSUs, only California Polytechnic State University in San Luis Obispo and San Diego State University are considered selective. Beyond California, all the Ivy League universities are considered selective. Many of the top small liberal arts colleges, such as Amherst, Bowdoin, and Macalester are also selective colleges. Even selective colleges can be further classified according to how selective they are.

Relative to less selective colleges, more selective colleges admit students who have higher test scores, and these colleges have lower admissions rates (Hoxby 2009; Hoxby and Avery 2012; Smith, Pender, and Howell 2013). A college's selectivity has a tangible impact on student experiences. Hoxby (2009) noted that since the 1960s there have been increasing disparities between more selective institutions and other institutions in regard to resources and subsidies for students. As of 2007, low-selectivity schools spend about $12,000 per student, whereas the highest-selectivity schools allocate resources to students to the tune of $92,000 per student. As Hoxby (2009) concluded, "The stakes associated with choosing a college are greater today than they were four decades ago. For very high-aptitude students, the stakes are much greater. The very large per-student resources and per-student subsidies at very selective colleges enable such students to make massive human capital investments if they are admitted" (116).

Due to the expansion and differentiation of the U.S. system of higher education, where students go to college matters as much as whether or not they go at all (Gladieux 2004). Relatedly, social class differences have emerged in where students begin college, whether they enroll full time, and their chances for completing a degree. Students from lower socioeconomic backgrounds, for example, are less likely than their more advantaged peers to start at a four-year institution, take a full course load, and complete a bachelor's degree (Alexander, Holupka, and Pallas 1987; Karen 2002; Cabrera, Burkum, and La Nasa 2005). Students from disadvantaged backgrounds are also more likely to enroll in public community colleges, a starting point from which the prospects for earning a bachelor's degree are low (McPherson and Schapiro 2006; Ayalon et al. 2008). Indeed, only one out of five students from the bottom socioeconomic quartile enrolled in a four-year institution within two years of high school graduation, compared to two out of three from the top income quartile (Gladieux 2004).

While attendance at community colleges and nonselective higher education institutions may impede students' ability to finish college, matriculation at a college of high quality eases passage through the system of higher education. Students who attend selective colleges are more likely to graduate on time, to receive a graduate or professional degree, and to have higher earnings compared to those who attend nonselective colleges (Bowen and Bok 2000; Carnevale and Rose 2004; Bowen, Chingos, and McPherson 2009). For instance, William Bowen and his colleagues (2009) found that high-achieving students have an 89 percent graduation rate when they attend colleges ranked as most selective, but just 59 percent when they attend colleges ranked as least selective. The most selective of these colleges are private institutions, and they tend to be residential, have relatively small enrollments, and have financial resources to afford smaller classes and more support services (Bowen and Bok 2000).

These different opportunities across selective colleges can have a dramatic impact on students' educational experiences. Indeed, research has shown that top private colleges spend more per student and subsidize student costs at a much higher rate than other selective colleges (Carnevale and Rose 2004; Hill and Winston 2006). In contrast, public selective colleges have lower graduation rates, due in part to larger enrollments and less assistance in the form of need-based financial aid (Bowen and Bok 2000). Among all selective colleges, less selective institutions typically have smaller budgets and lower spending per student (Hoxby 2009). This translates into less academic support, which has been shown to reduce graduation rates (Webber and Ehrenberg 2010).

Unsurprisingly, these disparate levels of investment lead to long-term advantages for those students who attend the private, highly selective colleges. For example, graduates of selective colleges disproportionately occupy political and economic leadership roles in society (McPherson and Schapiro 2006). This is especially the case for students who attend top private selective colleges, such as Ivy League universities and top liberal arts colleges. For instance, in one particularly prominent example, all the U.S. presidents over the last twenty years, and all the current Supreme Court Justices, attended highly selective private institutions (McPherson and Schapiro 2006).

Access to Elite Universities

The social and economic value of attending a highly selective college, especially a private college, cannot be understated. Thus it is important to understand how students end up in these colleges. Previous research has demonstrated that even among students of similar abilities there are systematic group differences based on social class background regarding access to different types of colleges (Karabel and Astin 1975; Hearn 1991; Lopez Turley, Santos, and Ceja 2007). For instance, while the influence of parents' education and income on the likelihood of students applying to any college has remained about the same across student cohorts, its influence on applying to a selective college has increased across cohorts (Lopez Turley et al. 2007). Indeed, only a small fraction (10 percent) of students at the nation's leading private college and universities come from the bottom 40 percent of the U.S. family income distribution. However, despite only representing 10 percent of the student population at these private colleges, more than 10 percent of those who score well—the highly able students—come from these low-income families (Hill and Winston 2006). This situation—where a student's academic credentials permit them access to a college or university that is more selective than the postsecondary alternative they end up choosing—is known as an academic undermatch (Smith, Pender, and Howell 2013; Hoxby and Avery 2012). This academic undermatch is more common among those students from families with low socioeconomic status families, those who live in rural areas, and those whose parents have no college degree (Smith, Pender, and Howell 2013).

Hoxby and Avery (2012) published an influential study where they found that the vast majority of high-achieving, low-income students do not apply to any selective college or university. Among the graduating high school students from 2008 that they looked at, the majority (53 percent) of low-income, high-achieving students exhibited what they called income-typical behavior—they applied to schools whose median standardized test scores are at least 15 percentiles below their own and to at least one nonselective college. Only a tiny portion (9 percent) applied to college in a manner that is somewhat close to what is recommended to their high-income counterparts. By comparison, this latter group—those from high-income families—applied to at least one match college, at least one safety college with median scores not more than 15 percentiles lower than their own, and zero nonselective colleges.

Other scholars have also demonstrated the prevalence of this kind of academic undermatch among low-income students. For example, Alexandria Radford (2013) published a study revealing how students from economically disadvantaged schools are less likely than their affluent peers to apply to selective institutions. Drawing on data from a survey of approximately 900 public high school valedictorians, Radford (2013) found that 50 percent of students with a low socioeconomic status (SES) and 42 percent of middle-SES valedictorians abandoned the possibility of attending a most-selective private college by not filing an application to at least one such institution (113). In contrast, only 20 percent of high-SES valedictorians eliminated this type of elite college from consideration. Radford (2013) concluded that to explain why low-income, high-achieving students are less likely to enroll at highly selective institutions, we need to recognize that the "the divergence by SES is set in motion in the application stage" (151).

While high academic achievement is what enables students to get into top selective colleges, it is not the only obstacle facing students from socioeconomically disadvantaged backgrounds. Even after academic credentials are taken into account, social class still affects where students apply and where they end up in college. Among high-achieving students from lower socioeconomic backgrounds who have the credentials to make them competitive applicants, many are not submitting applications to the nation's leading colleges and universities. Why this is the case is the focus of this book.

College Choice Decision-Making Frameworks

Two prevailing frameworks for understanding the decision making of individuals are rational choice theory and social reproduction theory. Both frameworks have been used to explain social class differences in the college application behaviors of students. The following sections review each of these frameworks and make the case for why they are inadequate for explaining the process by which social class shapes the college choices of students.

Rational Choice Theory

Rational choice models are popular among economists and scholars in other fields for making sense of how individuals make decisions. As such, they have served as a useful approach for scholars of higher education to examine how high school students decide where to apply to college. While there are several variants of rational choice models, what they have in common is their assumption that decision making involves an evaluation of the costs and benefits of engaging in some particular action. Applied to high school students' college choice decision making, rational choice models represent high school students as individuals choosing among different educational options on the basis of an evaluation of these options' costs and benefits (Breen and Goldthorpe 1997; Beattie 2002; Brand and Xie 2010). Rational choice scholars predict that prospective students decide whether to attend college and select among a range of institutions if their expected current and future benefits outweigh the anticipated costs (Grodsky and Jones 2007; Kim 2012).

While most applications of rational choice models to college choice decision making have primarily focused on costs and benefits in financial terms, a few have emphasized the importance of nonfinancial factors, such as perceived social fit with the college, its location, and its special academic programs (Hamrick and Hossler 1996; Dillon and Smith 2013). Consequently, there does not seem to be much agreement over what these costs and benefits are as different studies utilize different factors to represent the costs and benefits of colleges. Moreover, other rational models assert that both an assessment of costs and benefits and the probability of success influence what decisions students make (Breen and Goldthorpe 1997; Morgan 2005; Grodsky and Jones 2007).

Rational choice explanations about why low-income, high-achieving students are less likely to apply to elite institutions primarily center on the idea that these students lack two types of information: information about the different quality of colleges, and information about the financial costs and financial aid of these postsecondary institutions (Plank and Jordan 2001; Kelly and Schneider 2011; Hoxby and Turner 2013; Radford 2013; Smith, Pender, and Howell 2013). The former type of information refers to knowledge about the different types of college available—knowledge about one's own abilities relative to other college students, and knowledge about the consequences of attending colleges of different qualities (Dillon and Smith 2009). For instance, Hoxby and Avery (2012) concluded that low-income, high-achieving students rarely apply to selective colleges because they lack information about the availability of financial aid at such institutions that would help offset these colleges' high sticker prices. Stephen Plank and Will Jordan (2001) found that many low-SES high school students and their parents make decisions based on incomplete or inaccurate information about costs and available financial aid. As a consequence, the authors concluded that these students decide that some postsecondary schools are financially unfeasible based on their perceptions of prohibitive expenses and scarce aid. According to Dillion and Smith (2009), while both information and finances play a role in predicting which students are most likely to end up poorly matched with their college, lack of information about the different types of college is the more important constraint.

The rational choice approach provides a useful perspective for understanding how high school students decide where to apply and attend college. It offers an important lens for grasping the role that the absence of accurate information about differences in college quality and financial costs of postsecondary educational institutions play in relegating high-achieving, low-income students to colleges whose academic reputation is well below that of these students' ability level. However, rational choice models do not adequately address how differences in social background affect how students use whatever information they have available to make decisions. Moreover, to assume that higher-income students make more rational decisions because they have access to a greater quantity and quality of information about higher education ignores whether such information actually figures into the decision making of these students.

Social Reproduction Theory

While rational choice scholars conceive of decision making as the result of rational utilitarian choices made by actors occupying different class positions, other scholars, including social reproduction theorists associated with Pierre

Bourdieu, argue that some of these decisions can be explained largely in terms of unconscious cultural processes that bring social destination into conformity with social origin (Bourdieu 1990; Hatcher 1998; Bourdieu 1999). Social reproduction scholars contend that for some students, particularly those from socioeconomically advantaged families, the decision of whether to attend college or where to apply to college is not based on an evaluation of the costs and benefits of different options. Instead, it is more like a nondecision in that it is assumed or taken for granted by these students and their families that they will attend college after high school or that they will only apply to a select group of colleges. Other options or alternatives are not even considered by these students.

For instance, Jennie Brand and Yu Xie (2010) argued that the college decision is not a straightforward balancing of costs and returns; instead, it is heavily influenced by cultural and social circumstances. Indeed, some individuals make decisions or engage in particular actions without the need to consciously resort to some underlying rational logic (McDonough 1997; Ball et al. 2002). This understanding of decision making as being unconscious is influenced by Bourdieu's concept of habitus, which refers to a set of dispositions acquired through a gradual process that predisposes individuals to make their actions and decisions conform to the objective conditions of their class positions (Bourdieu 1999). According to Bourdieu (1990; 1999), individuals can make decisions or engage in particular actions without the need to consciously resort to some underlying rational logic as to why that path of action is appropriate. Rather, they follow their dispositions, which allow them to make reasonable and rational decisions because these dispositions are compatible with the conditions of their social and economic environment. While the process used to make these decisions may not seem rational—in that individuals do not deliberately calculate the costs and benefits of different options—the decision itself is often rational in that it is the one that best serves the interests of individuals in light of the constraints and opportunities present in their social environment (Bourdieu 1990; 1999).

While Bourdieu's concept of habitus seems to suggest that individuals need not consciously resort to some underlying rational logic to make decisions, it is incorrect to assume that this applies to every decision. Instead, habitus is most relevant to explaining typical, routine actions, and not necessarily major decisions. Yet, what one social or economic group deems as routine (e.g., attending college) may not seem so natural to other groups. As Richard Hatcher (1998) pointed out while highlighting the distinction between rational choice and habitus, "Rational choice theory has concerned itself with 'choice' in terms of key institutional transition points. The concept of habitus addresses not the exceptional but the routine" (21).

A number of studies have used the concept of habitus in their examination of class differences in college decision-making behavior. Patricia McDonough (1997), for example, developed the concept of organizational habitus, defined as the impact of a social class culture through an intermediate organization (e.g., high school), to describe the process by which schools structure students' college choices. The concept of organizational habitus explains how individuals' decisions exist within the boundaries set by organizations—for instance, different schools offer different views of the college opportunity structure. Similarly, Stephen Ball and colleagues (2002) argued that the institutional habitus of schools, which consists of embedded perceptions and expectations, makes certain choices obvious and others unthinkable. As they note, "Habitus [is] evident here in its inexplicitness" (Ball et al. 2002, 58). For instance, in interviews with students from well-to-do families about college choices, the starting point was whether or not to attend a particular prestigious university, rather than a consideration of different college options (Ball et al. 2002). Furthermore, other scholars have demonstrated how college choices are tied to socialization and the development of an identity, showing how parents and schools cultivated an identity among high-achieving students as "selective college goers," such that "attending a four-year, highly selective college is both an expectation and an identity marker, and increasingly the 'norm' for those at the top of the Cannondale [school] class" (Weiss, Cipollone, and Jenkins 2014, 64). As a result, the decision to apply to particular colleges— selective ones—was not a deliberate decision for some students; instead, it was something students took for granted given their identity.

Like rational-choice theory, social reproduction theory provides an important approach to understanding college selection. However, it too has limits for this. A number of scholars have critiqued social reproduction theory for its overly social deterministic view of behavior; it does not sufficiently address how it is that individuals can engage in decisions or practices that deviate from their habitus. Moreover, the role of deliberate decision making is underestimated by social reproduction theory (Nash 1990; Hatcher 1998).

Though the rational choice and social reproduction frameworks each provide a different perspective at understanding the decision-making process, they have limitations. By conceptualizing decision making as primarily an individual endeavor, rational choice explanations overlook how students are embedded in social or cultural contexts that may render some choices more likely than others. Social reproduction theory, on the other hand, offers an overly structural and deterministic account that leaves little room for understanding how individuals can diverge from what is expected in their social or cultural environments. Each framework tells us more about students' social environments or the nature of their decision making and less about the process by which social class gives rise to different types of decision making.

Culture and Cognition Framework

Given the limitations of these two frameworks for understanding the college-selection process, there is a need for another framework that can explain how the constraints or opportunities in the social environment influence students' understandings of college and the decisions they make. This book draws on a culture and cognition framework to address this gap in the literature. This framework depicts decision making not as being either deliberate (rational) or unconscious (habitus), but rather based on how people perceive the world and how they act on those perceptions (Lamont et al. 2014). People from different structural positions attach different meanings to the same phenomenon, which then leads them to act in different ways in response. Applied to the college choice decision-making process, this framework contends that it is not simply a matter of having access to information but also of how students from different structural positions (e.g., social class backgrounds) make sense of this information within the context of their own understandings of higher education.

A culture and cognition framework provides analytical leverage over rational choice and habitus because it takes into account both the individual and the structural environment. It also provides the conceptual tools to uncover the processes by which structure and culture influence individual choices. By focusing on the subjective understandings of individuals, this framework enables an analysis of how social class–based experiences inform students' understandings of higher education and how students employ those understandings in making college application decisions.

A culture and cognition framework reflects the changes in the study of culture, which has shifted from a focus on values and motives behind social action to a series of conceptual tools that highlight the different ways in which culture enables or constrains social action. Summarizing these new approaches to the study of culture, Stephen Vaisey (2010) writes, "These 'new culture' scholars have rejected the idea that culture operates by shaping motives and instead argue that culture makes some actions possible and others difficult or impossible by constituting one's repertoire of skills and knowledge" (78). Moreover, this new approach toward the study of culture has distanced itself from viewing culture as a coherent, consistent system and has instead emphasized the fragmented nature of culture (DiMaggio 1997). Consequently, this new approach to the study of culture has produced multiple definitions, resulting in six different, but sometimes overlapping, perspectives on how culture shapes social action. These six different concepts—frames, repertoires, narratives, symbolic boundaries, cultural capital, and institution—each highlight particular aspects of culture that make some actions more likely than others. This book draws on three of these concepts—frames, narratives, and institutions—to explain how social class shapes the college choice decision-making process.

Frames

Research studies that draw on cultural frames rely on a conception that can be traced back to the works of Erving Goffman (1974) and the social movement literature (Benford and Snow 2000). For Goffman, frames represent "schemata of interpretation" that allow individuals to "locate, perceive, identify, and label" occurrences within their life and the larger society (1974, 21). Benford and Snow (2000) similarly define frames as "an interpretive [schema] that simplifies and condenses the 'world out there' by selectively punctuating and encoding objects, situations, events, experiences, and sequences of actions within one's present or past environment" (80). Both of these definitions emphasize the importance of interpretation in how people perceive and act on the world. The idea behind the concept of frames is that people's perception of events shapes how they respond to them. Individuals may perceive the same events differently based on the different prior understandings and experiences they bring to the situation. By highlighting certain aspects of social life and hiding or blocking others, "frames can be thought of as a lens through which we observe and interpret social life" (Small, Harding, and Lamont 2010).

Many scholars have used the concept of frames to uncover the ways in which specific events and circumstances affect people and their decision making. Examining participation in a Latino housing project, for example, Mario Small (2002) showed that individuals' descriptions or framings of their neighborhood influenced whether they participated in the local activities of the neighborhood. Those who conceived of the neighborhood as a community, a neighborhood with a significant history of political and social involvement, continued that tradition by participating in local activities. Meanwhile, individuals who perceived the neighborhood as merely projects, a low-income area with no notable history, did not participate. David Harding (2007) examined frames regarding teenage pregnancy in disadvantaged neighborhoods and finds the existence of both mainstream frames that highlight the potential for a teenage pregnancy to derail schooling, and alternative frames that highlight the adult social status that comes with childbearing. By noting the existence of these multiple frames, Harding (2007) argued that adolescents in disadvantaged neighborhoods have more options for conceiving of their circumstances, which can have an impact on teenage pregnancies. In another example for how frames can be employed to shed light on specific social phenomena, Alfred Young (2004) found that the relative degree of isolation of Black men shaped their framing or interpretation of the issues of stratification, inequality, and prospects for mobility. The men who experienced greater social exposure across race and class lines tended to emphasize social conditions. The more socially isolated men tended to blame Black men themselves for their plight.

A number of studies by scholars working in the field of education have contributed to a greater understanding of the role of frames in shaping the behaviors of high school students. While these studies do not always explicitly draw on or engage with the concept of frames, their findings help to shed light on how interpretations can constrain or enable certain actions. Signithia Fordham and John Ogbu (1986) argued that how Black students perceive academic achievement shapes the amount of effort they exert in school. They assert that due to structural discrimination in the form of inferior schooling and job ceiling, some Black Americans develop a coping mechanism that associates academic achievement with "acting white." This framing of academic achievement as "acting white" causes a social and psychological situation that diminishes Black students' academic effort and thus leads to underachievement. While their "acting white" thesis has been debunked by many researchers as a cause of Black underachievement (Tyson, Darity Jr., and Castellino 2005; Carter 2006), Fordham and Ogbu's (1986) focus on how different interpretations of academic achievement may give rise to different behaviors was a valuable contribution to the conception of culture as frames.

Jay MacLeod's (1987) study of two teenage male groups reveals that the group which framed the opportunity structure as essentially an open one that rewarded hard work and effort was more integrated in schools and positive about the future. Members of the other group, which framed the opportunity structure as closed due to class-based obstacles, were more likely to drop out of school and were more despondent about their future. These studies point to the existence of different frames for interpreting the same social phenomenon, and how certain frames increase the likelihood of one action over others. By understanding the frames that students of different social class backgrounds use to make decisions about pursuing higher education, we can gain a better understanding about the way students undertake their decision making during the college selection process.

Narratives

In addition to frames, I also draw on the concept of narratives to help shed light on the decision-making process of students. While narratives are similar to frames in that they both cognitively shape how people interpret their social world, narratives are stories with a "causally-linked sequence of events" (Small, Harding, and Lamont 2010). They have a beginning, middle, and ending and are stories that people tell which express how they make sense of their lives. Narratives consist of three elements (Ewick and Silbey 2003). First, a narrative relies on some form of selective appropriation of past events and characters. Second, within a narrative the events must be temporally ordered. This quality of narrative requires that the selected events be presented with a beginning, a middle, and an end. Third, the events and characters must be related to one another and to some overarching structure, often to an opposition or struggle. The temporal and structural ordering ensure both narrative closure and narrative causality, which is an account about how and why the events occurred as they did.

Narratives provide a glimpse into how individuals view themselves in relation to others and are therefore central to how individuals construct social identities (Abelmann 1997; Small, Harding, and Lamont 2010). Individuals choose actions that are consistent with their personal identities and personal narratives. People act, or do not act, in part according to how they understand their place in any number of given narratives—however fragmented, contradictory, or partial (Somers 1994). According to Michelle Lamont and Mario Small (2008), "This perspective shows that action is not an automatic response to incentive: it is made possible within the context of narratives around which people make sense of their lives" (84).

A narrative approach assumes that people are guided to act by the structural and cultural relationships in which they are embedded and by the stories through which they constitute their identities (Somers 1994). The narratives people tell about themselves and others reveal how they make sense of their experiences, constraints, and opportunities. As Patricia Ewick and Susan Silbey (2003) describe it, narratives "locate characters in time and space, describing both what enables and what constrains action . . . they point to the sources and limits of agency that exist within social structure" (1342). Narratives reveal the subject's consciousness of how opportunities and constraints are embedded in the normally taken for granted structures of social action. The concept of narratives contributes to a better understanding of the college choice decision-making process by highlighting how students make decisions that reflect the narratives they have about themselves and the social world.

Institutions

In addition to frames and narratives, the concept of institutions represents another important tool to explain students' college selection process. The concept of institution helps capture what organizations are and how they operate. *Institutions* refers to the "formal and informal rules, procedures, routines, and norms, as socially shared cognitive and interpretative schemas, or more narrowly yet, as formal organizations" (Lamont and Small 2008, 98). This definition consists of three conceptions of institutions, each of which is helpful to note here and which this book draws on: as formal rules of behavior that are codified as laws or regulations, as norms of appropriate behavior that are codified through informal sanctions, and as taken-for-granted understandings that structure how individuals perceive their circumstances (Small, Harding, and Lamont 2010). The three conceptions of institutions allow researchers to examine the different ways in which organizations influence the way individuals think and behave. While each conception emphasizes a different aspect of examination, what they all have in common is the idea that organizations operate via socially shared cognitive and interpretive schemas. In other words, within each organization, there are shared systems of rules and understandings (e.g., schemas) that influence how individuals make sense of their surroundings and their decisions. The concept of institutions thus draws our attention to the ways in which action is structured by shared systems of understandings and rules in organizational settings (Dimaggio and Powell 1991).

Organizations structure action through the schemas they impart to individuals. Socially shared cognitive and interpretive schemas involve sorting individuals, groups, or things into categories that are arranged, usually, within a hierarchy. The consequence is the creation of shared classification systems through which individuals perceive and make sense of their environment (Lamont et al. 2014). This sorting process both opens and closes opportunities, and it enables and constrains individuals' life course trajectories. The process of evaluation results in one or more hierarchies that separate appealing options from less desirable ones. As Michelle Lamont and colleagues (2014) describe it, "Evaluation is a process that results in winners and losers, for example, through rankings, or the differential allocation of desirable resources" (594).

Applied to the college-choice decision making, schemas reflect the product of a process of categorization, evaluation, and legitimation of college options within high schools and college preparation programs. Schemas represent the conceptual tool that enables an analysis of how high schools and academic programs shape students' decision making by way of the configuration of colleges that are provided to students within the organizational setting. This book, by looking at schools and programs through the institutional lens, specifically the concept of schemas, identifies the configuration of colleges presented to students in their high schools or programs, describes how the structure or conditions of each organization give rise to this specific configuration, and then elaborates on the process by which these configurations of colleges interact with students' own experiences and understandings to shape their college application choices.

Data Collection

The research in this book is based on an analysis of forty-six in-depth interviews with high-achieving students from the San Francisco Bay Area who were in their senior year in high school. To be considered high-achieving, students needed to have SAT scores above 1260 or ACT scores above 28 and an unweighted GPA of at least 3.7. These criteria are similar to the ones used by

Hoxby and Avery (2012) in their definition of a high-achieving student: an individual whose ACT or SAT I test scores put them in the 90th percentile of all test takers and whose average GPA is A— or above. Hoxby and Avery's (2012) cutoff for the SAT I was 1300 and 29 for the ACT.

Higher-SES students were recruited primarily from two schools through the use of snowball sampling. At each of the two high schools, I reached out to students in school clubs and via flyers that were posted on school campus, resulting in twenty interviews. The remaining three higher-SES students from this study were recruited via flyers that I posted around the cities of Berkeley and Oakland. Lower-SES students were recruited primarily from their participation in several college-preparation programs for low-income and first-generation college students. A handful of lower-SES students were recruited through their schools by way of teachers forwarding my research to their students.

Most students were interviewed twice, with the first interview being the primary one that inquired about how students applied to college and the second one being the follow-up about where students will attend college. The first interview consisted of questions about students' individual and family background, their approach to higher education, their preparation for college, their exploration of colleges, and lastly, where they applied to colleges. These interviews were conducted at libraries and cafés. They lasted anywhere from 45 minutes to 2.5 hours, but most averaged 1.5 hours. The second interview, which was primarily about where students decided to attend college, was over the phone and lasted anywhere between 15 and 30 minutes.

Twenty-three of the research participants were categorized as lower-SES and twenty-three were categorized as higher-SES. Lower-SES students were defined as students whose parents had not completed a bachelor's degree and were not working in a professional occupation. Among lower-SES students, all but three students had parental incomes under $50,000. These three students had family incomes between $50,000 and $75,000. These students were still categorized as lower-SES based on the lack of a higher-education degree and the absence of a professional occupation among the parents. Moreover, these students participated in programs for socioeconomically disadvantaged students. Consequently, lower-SES students in this research refers to poor, low-income, working-class, and first-generation college students.

Higher-SES students were defined as those students for whom at least one parent had a bachelor's degree or higher and was working in a professional occupation. With the exception of two students, higher-SES students had family incomes above $75,000. One student reported his family income as between $25,000 and $50,000 and the other stated his family income was between $50,000 and $75,000. These two students were still categorized as higher-SES students based on the backgrounds and current circumstances of their parents. One student was living in an affluent community; both of his parents were college graduates from China, but only his father was currently working. The other student also attended school in an affluent area; his parents were both college graduates, but his father was forced into retirement, resulting in his mother being the only working adult. As a result, higher-SES students are from families that are considered middle- and upper-middle class.

Among the lower-SES sample, there were three African Americans, fifteen Asian Americans, and five Hispanics. The higher-SES sample included one Hispanic, twelve Asian Americans, eight whites, and two multiracial students. There were more females than males in each SES group. Except for the three African American students and seven (out of eight) white students, all other students in the study had at least one parent who was an immigrant. Some of these students are themselves immigrants. All names used in this research are pseudonyms.

To analyze my data, I transcribed and then coded the interviews. The codes were developed to reflect the areas of inquiry in my in-depth interview questionnaire. The areas of interest included student background and activities, family background, high school description, and student experiences in different phases of the college choice decision-making process—from college exploration and college preparation to college application. My codes were developed to capture students' responses to these areas of interest. For instance, codes such as family background, family involvement, and family obligations were used to capture the influences of the family on the lives and decision making of students. In another instance, when it came to students' responses regarding their criteria for selecting where they would submit college applications, I applied codes that reflect the different factors, such as distance, application requirements, admission requirements, college size, and rankings.

Data analysis after the coding process consisted of the identification of social class differences in how students applied to college. I examined the frequency and content of codes by social class. I also focused on the different factors, such as family, schools, programs, and community, in shaping student experiences as they explored colleges, prepared for college, and applied to college. While the brunt of the analysis took place after the coding process, I also drew upon the memos that I wrote at different stages of the data collection process. Throughout the interview process, I wrote memos that summarized patterns around how students applied to college, and how these patterns differed by social class. Together, these memos and the analysis of codes pointed me toward how schools, college preparation programs, and families play pivotal roles in shaping where students apply to college. Although the analyses yielded themes around how students approached the college choice decision-making process, it was the concepts from the culture and cognition framework that informed how I interpreted the process by which social class gave rise to differences in decision making.

How Social Class Matters for College Choices

When comparing the application decisions of high-achieving students from lower- and higher-SES backgrounds, what distinguishes the college application choices of one group from the other is not the selectivity of the colleges, but the geography and type of selective colleges. Students from lower-SES backgrounds tended to limit their choices of colleges to those within California, whereas students from higher-SES backgrounds applied to top colleges across the United States. As table 1 shows, among twenty-three lower-SES students, only seven applied out of state. In contrast, higher-SES students applied to in-state colleges as well, but they also submitted applications to out-of-state universities at a much higher rate. Out of twenty-three higher-SES students, twenty-one students applied to out-of-state colleges. By only applying to colleges close to home and in California, lower-SES students applied primarily to large public selective universities (University of California [UC] universities) and nonselective public colleges (California State University [CSU] colleges). In contrast, higher-SES students applied to selective private colleges across the country, such as Ivy League universities, top liberal arts colleges on the East Coast and in the Midwest, and major public and private research universities across the United States.

The fact that application to selective colleges was not affected by the social class backgrounds of students is due to the public higher education system in California, which comprises three tiers of colleges. The top tier is the UC system, which has nine undergraduate campuses and offers admission to one of its campuses to any high school senior in the state who graduates in the top eighth (12.5 percent) of their high school's graduating class. All but two of the UCs are selective colleges. Every student in this study, regardless of their social class background, applied to the UCs, and their applications included at least one selective UC campus. The other two tiers are the California State Universities

Table 1
Social class and types of colleges applied to

	Total subjects	# Applied to in-state colleges	# Applied to out-of-state colleges	# Applied to at least one out-of-state liberal arts college	#Applied to at least one Ivy League university
Higher-SES students	23	23	21	14	15
Lower-SES students	23	23	7	4	3

(CSUs), which admit the top third (33 percent) of California's high school graduates, and the community colleges (CCs), which are open to any individual with a high school diploma or its equivalent. Only two colleges in the CSU system are considered selective, whereas none of the two-year community colleges are considered selective colleges. Due to the selectivity of a handful of California's UC campuses, California represents a best-case scenario for socioeconomically disadvantaged students in that they are likely to apply to at least one selective college just by submitting applications to the top in-state public universities.

Despite the fact that lower-SES students applied to selective colleges, they did not apply to the same types of selective colleges as their higher-SES counterparts. By limiting themselves to California colleges, many lower-SES students applied to more nonselective colleges and passed up on private selective colleges, particularly Ivy League and small liberal arts colleges. The resources and benefits of attending a selective private college are more pronounced than those available at a selective public university. At selective private research universities and small liberal arts colleges, the student bodies are much smaller, and these colleges spend more per student than do selective public universities (Carnevale and Rose 2004; Hoxby 2009; Hoxby and Avery 2012). As a result, at selective private colleges, the class sizes are smaller, students have more opportunities for interactions with their faculty, there are greater opportunities for students to do research independently or with faculty members (Bowen and Bok 2000; Hill and Winston 2006; Hoxby and Avery 2012). Moreover, individuals who attend selective private universities with small enrollments have significantly higher earnings later on in life when compared to those who attend selective public universities (Brewer, Eide, and Ehrenberg 1999).

Social class differences affect where students apply to college, as I show in this book, because of the way high schools and college preparation programs shape the choices of students by establishing boundaries around which colleges they consider appropriate for their students. High schools and college preparation programs represented organizations that provided students with schemas to help them narrow down college options to a manageable set. What was considered appropriate varied by the mission of the organization and the population of subjects served. For instance, higher-SES students attended high schools in which every student was expected to go on to a four-year college. The inevitability of college was supported by a school environment in which students were presented with a *selective college anywhere* schema by which selective colleges, especially private ones, from across the country (e.g., top UCs, selective private liberal arts colleges, and Ivy League universities) were promoted, whereas low-ranked and nonselective colleges (e.g., CSUs, two-year colleges, and low-ranked UCs—all within the state) were stigmatized.

In contrast to higher-SES students, most lower-SES students attended high schools and participated in college preparation programs in which a four-year college was among one of multiple post–high school options. As a result, these students were exposed to a configuration of colleges that reflected an *any postsecondary education* schema or an *in-state four-year college* schema. In the *any postsecondary education* schema, students were encouraged to pursue any additional education after high school, whether it was vocational/trade schools, two-year colleges, or four-year colleges. In the *in-state four-year college* schema, any type of four-year colleges (e.g., UCs and CSUs), regardless of selectivity or rankings, was emphasized, whereas two-year and vocational schools were discouraged. In both of these configurations, out-of-state colleges were rarely discussed and were essentially ignored. As a result, most lower-SES students were limited to deciding among local and in-state California colleges, while their higher-SES peers considered colleges across the country.

Whereas high schools and programs shaped the colleges to which students were exposed, family upbringing and experiences also notably influenced college choices through their impact on students' understandings of college and their perceptions of how much autonomy they had over their decision making. The concept of narratives captured how this process unfolded over time through a multitude of experiences. When discussing their decision-making processes, higher-SES students presented a *narrative of independence* regarding what they had done to prepare for college and where to apply. They emphasized aspects of their upbringing and experiences that demonstrated how they exercised initiative in making decisions about the activities in which they should participate. They downplayed the influence of their parents in making these decisions, and they saw themselves as individuals who were autonomous in choosing their directions and college options. As a result, most higher-SES students framed college as an opportunity to leave their families and immerse themselves in a new environment in a different part of the country.

Most lower-SES students, on the other hand, understood college as a continuation of family interdependence, and they viewed making decisions about college as an undertaking that required taking into account the real and perceived needs and wishes of the family. These students spoke of experiences and considerations that reflected a *narrative of interdependence* between themselves and their parents that was grounded in the mutual concern that they have for one another as the prospect of college loomed. This narrative included stories that reflected some combination of students' awareness of the sacrifices and struggles of their parents to support the family, students' family responsibilities while in high school, students' anticipation of their role in the health and success of their family in the future, and parental pressures for students to stay close to home for college. Due to these experiences, students recognized the importance of mutual support between themselves and their parents in any future success, reinforcing the belief that the fate of students and parents was intertwined. As a result, most lower-SES students framed college as a continuation of family interdependence, a narrative that placed spatial restrictions on their consideration of colleges.

Due to social class influences grounded in high schools, academic programs, and family factors, higher-SES students were more likely to apply to selective private universities in other parts of the country, whereas lower-SES students tended to limit their choices to colleges—both selective and nonselective—closer to home. By focusing on the decision-making process among students, I show how students' decisions about which college to apply to are not merely a straightforward consideration of the costs and benefits of various college options, or even a function of the informational context available to them. Instead these decisions are also intimately linked to students' social class upbringing and experiences.

While the underlying issue in this book is that of social class, I also show that a student's race, gender, and immigrant background add additional layers of complexity to the college decision-making process. Students' multifaceted identity and experiences shaped how they thought about their choices as well as how others (teachers and parents) reacted to their choices. Among lower-SES students, children of immigrants felt obligated to consider the needs of their family in their decision making, something reflected in their narratives of interdependence. Aside from obligations, a couple of Hispanic students brought up the immigration status of their parents as potential obstacles in their consideration of out-of-state colleges. Lower-SES female students were typically more involved with household duties, and they faced stronger resistance from their families when they considered colleges far from home. Lower-SES Asian American students were more likely to attend high schools of relatively better quality than their Hispanic and African American peers; moreover, they were more likely to participate in programs that sought to place socioeconomically disadvantaged students in the nation's leading colleges and universities. These complexities are highlighted in the relevant chapters.

Overview of the Book

Chapter 1 examines how students from different social class backgrounds decide that they will attend college upon their completion of high school. I show that higher-SES students framed college attendance as inevitable and a natural progression of schooling. As a result, the decision to attend college required little deliberation, and higher-SES students assumed from a very young age that they would attend college. This was because higher-SES students grew up in families and communities in which almost every adult had completed college. In contrast, most lower-SES students framed college as one of multiple options.

The completion of high school represented a key transitional point. As such, the decision to attend college was often one that had to be contemplated as the right path. This was because lower-SES students grew up in families and communities in which college was one of several pathways available to them after high school. Consequently, the decision to attend college actually represented a conscious decision that students had to justify as the right path for them. Indeed, most lower-SES students pointed to key moments in middle or high school when they decided that they would attend college based on knowledge about colleges or experiences in college environments.

Chapter 2 analyzes the preparation approaches of students and the various types of activities students participated in as they readied themselves for college. The approaches and the activities represented the efforts of students to position themselves to be competitive applicants for college as well as to be successful once they were in college. The approach of lower-SES students revolved around developing their competence to succeed in college and at projecting an identity of a well-rounded student. They discussed efforts to cultivate social and academic skills that would enable them to thrive in college. They also wanted to project an image of a student who was strong in academics and committed to interests beyond the classroom. In contrast, the approach of higher-SES students was driven by the desire to stand out among their peers. Higher-SES students sought to engage in activities that they believed distinguished themselves from others. This strategy centered as much on the activities they engaged in as it did on how they rationalized their involvement. In discussing their approach and involvement, higher-SES students frequently emphasized how they were unique from others in what they did or in how they did it—their involvement was framed as a reflection of their individual passion and personal autonomy.

Chapters 3 and 4 tackle the question of how social class shapes whether students apply to out-of-state colleges. Chapter 3 shows that high schools and college preparation programs shape the choices of students by establishing boundaries around which colleges are considered appropriate for students. Higher-SES students attended high schools in which competitive and highly ranked colleges in California and across the country were viewed as appropriate options. As a result, applications to out-of-state colleges were a common occurrence among higher-SES students. In contrast, most lower-SES students attended schools and participated in college preparation programs that presented them only with colleges in California. Some lower-SES students, specifically those in better resourced schools and those in programs geared toward getting high-achieving students into the top colleges across the country, were more likely to be exposed to a schema of colleges that included out-of-state colleges. However, being presented with a configuration of colleges that included out-of-state colleges was often not enough to get some lower-SES students to submit applications to those colleges. Lower-SES students who did apply to out-of-state colleges tended to have experiences in out-of-state environments or positive experiences with higher-SES students in better-resourced high schools. These experiences were instrumental in shaping their desire to apply to out-of-state colleges.

Chapter 4 shows that family upbringing and experiences influence college choices through their impact on students' understandings of college and their perceptions of how much autonomy they have over their decision making. Adopting narratives of interdependence or independence, students chose to present stories to answer questions about who they were and where they were heading. Lower-SES students spoke about dealing with family struggles and structural constraints, whereas higher-SES students told stories of how their parents set them up to make decisions about what they want to do growing up. Students were not just speaking about a single point in time. They referenced their experiences and upbringing during childhood, throughout middle and high school, and up to the point when they decided where to apply to college. While the overarching theme of the narrative among higher-SES students was that of autonomy, it was that of constraints grounded in child/parent interdependence for lower-SES students. This focus on interdependence limited lower-SES students to applying to colleges close to home in California. In contrast, higher-SES students highlighted the initiative and autonomy they had in their lives, which enabled them to consider applying to colleges across the country.

The conclusion reviews the contributions of each of the three concepts in advancing our understanding of the influences of social class on the decision making of individuals. It also examines the implications of the research in this book on the persistence of social inequality. I argue that our efforts at closing the academic achievement gap within schools should work in concert with efforts to reduce the social class gap in experiences and opportunities outside the classroom. If there is one lesson to be taken from this book, it is that academic achievement alone will not reduce social inequality. Finally, I discuss potential interventions that can encourage higher numbers of lower-SES, high-achieving students to apply to the nation's top colleges and universities.

1

Frames of College Attendance

● ●

> I was always skeptical that I would get into college. Everyone made it seem like it's something that you probably can't reach. What really hit me that I was going to go to college was that moment when I hit the accept button to [the University of California] Davis and I was like I am going to college. (Natalie, lower-SES Chinese American student)

> I always expected to go to college. I knew that I would probably go to college and go through what everyone else was doing. Apply to college because there's a stigma against not going to college. (Emily, higher-SES Chinese American student)

I begin this chapter with two quotes that highlight the different moments when two students of divergent social class backgrounds became certain that they would continue on to college after high school. Though all students in this research were college bound, and all submitted college applications, the process by which they reached the decision to pursue higher education differed according to their social class backgrounds. These quotes from Natalie and Emily reveal—and the experiences of other students in this study also underscore—that there is a significant difference between the timing and the manner in which lower-SES students and higher-SES students expressed certainty about their matriculation to college. Unlike lower-SES students, higher-SES students frequently noted that they had felt this certainty from a very young age. Among higher-SES students, the decision to continue on to college represented a nondecision because college attendance was not something to be deliberated upon but rather something that was assumed to occur. For higher-SES students, college represented merely another step in their schooling; as a result, it did not warrant the weighing of different post–high school options.

Unlike higher-SES students, most lower-SES students came to develop a commitment to college attendance later during their adolescent years. Lower-SES students referenced specific points in middle and high school when they became certain that they would go on to college. These moments reflected growing confidence at their likely satisfaction from going to college, and college's accessibility to them. Lower-SES students needed confirmation that they would enjoy the social environments of college and that they would be able to gain admission into college. These forms of knowledge, experience, and understanding came about largely through the intervention of extra-familial factors, such as teachers, academic programs, and college preparation programs.

The frames that students from different social class backgrounds drew on to make sense of higher education explained why some individuals engaged in a conscious decision about college attendance, whereas others took it for granted. For example, higher-SES students framed college as inevitable and a natural progression of schooling. As a result, the decision to attend college required little deliberation and students assumed from a very young age that they would attend college. College was the only option after high school. It was not up to students to decide whether college was the right path. This was because higher-SES students grew up in families and communities in which almost every adult had completed college. In contrast, lower-SES students grew up in families and environments in which college was one of several options available to them after high school. As a result, most lower-SES students framed college as one of multiple options. The completion of high school represented a key transitional point, and the decision to attend college was one that had to be decided on as the right path. Indeed, most lower-SES students pointed to key moments in middle or high school when they decided that they would attend college based on knowledge about colleges or experiences in college environments.

While the structure of students' decision making about college attendance differed based on their social class backgrounds, both higher-SES and lower-SES students drew on overlapping rationales to make sense of why they were going to pursue higher education. Whereas frames reflect how students thought about or interpreted the transition to college, rationales represent their justification or reasoning for their decision to go to college. One rationale was the internalization of expectations from adults. For higher-SES students, this was the internalization of an implicit expectation about college attendance—primarily from their family. They observed that their parents and other adults around them had attended college, and they came to expect this for themselves without anyone explicitly telling them. For lower-SES students, this internalization was primarily due to explicit expectations from adults like parents and academic staff or through participation in academic programs. A second rationale was linking college completion to social and economic mobility; students who referenced this rationale discussed how a college degree was the key to good jobs and a happy life—a social mobility rationale. A third rationale was that through accumulated knowledge about college and experiences on college campuses, students learned that college could be an enjoyable experience, socially or academically. This was the college satisfaction rationale. Finally, the fourth rationale was that by learning more about college requirements, students became aware that they were eligible or had a very good chance of gaining admission into a four-year college—what I call the academic evaluation rationale.

Although students relied on these kinds of overlapping rationales for why they would attend college, because of their different frames of college attendance, these rationales played different roles in each group's decision-making process. Whereas lower-SES students relied on these rationales to explain how they came to the decision that college was the right path for them, higher-SES students drew on the rationales to justify their taken-for-granted attitude toward college attendance.

College as One of Multiple Options

Most lower-SES students framed college as one of multiple options, and this frame of higher education was found in the doubts, hesitancy, and uncertainties that they expressed regarding college attendance. Some students did not know if college would be right for them. Others were not sure if they could get into college. The options other than college were revealed in lower-SES students' discussions about what non-college-educated adults in their communities and families did for a living. Discussing how these adults' paths influenced their own showed that lower-SES students considered other options before college became a certainty. The elimination of these other paths was evidence of their view of college as being one of multiple options.

Even though some lower-SES students had older siblings who had gone to college, these students' knowledge of college remained limited as they were growing up, just as it did for most lower-SES students. As such, lower-SES students relied on extrafamilial factors to convince them that college was the path for them; these students needed affirmation beyond the family. One group of students came to this conclusion through the internalization of expectations from teachers and academic program staff. For these individuals, the expectation of college from someone outside the family was sufficient to motivate them to attend college. Most students, however, needed to learn more about the college process and to gain some familiarity with college environments. Others needed confirmation that they had the necessary academic credentials to be accepted into college. In contrast to the majority of lower-SES students, a handful of lower-SES students expressed that the expectations of a parent (or parents) had solidified their decision to pursue higher education.

The following sections further examine each of these different influences for lower-SES students. Specifically, students' responses are organized into the different rationales that they drew on to explain how they became certain that they would pursue higher education. Together, they show that, for most lower-SES students, the decision to attend college was something that they had to arrive at through the accumulation of knowledge and experiences during adolescence.

Internalization of Expectations from Participation in Academic Programs

For lower-SES students, academic programs played a key role in creating the conditions in which they could increasingly accept the idea that college was the right path for them. Several lower-SES students decided that they would attend college as a result of their participation in academic enrichment programs in elementary and middle school. For these students, who knew very little about college before attending, participation in these programs fostered key expectations that they would attend college, and they came to internalize the expectation that college was the path for them. These students were primarily Asian Americans. Asian American parents frequently learned about these academic programs for their young children through their children's schools and their ethnic social networks. These programs facilitated their students' attachment to higher education. John, a Vietnamese American, was one such student. Neither of his parents had completed college, but he had three older siblings who had gone on to college. John's discussion about his parents' occupations in the restaurant industry and their expectations revealed his frame about higher education: "They [my parents] know they don't want me to have these lifestyles. They want me to escape this community. . . . Because I was still so young, it sort of shaped the way I saw school and that I needed to do good in school because it was going to be my escape."

The fact that John had to consciously eliminate the path his parents took, which is physically demanding, low-wage work, showed that he recognized that other paths were possible, even if they were not something that he wanted to pursue. Despite committing himself to doing well in school, John only became certain of college attendance later on during his middle school years. Through the recommendation of an elementary school teacher, John's parents enrolled him in a summer academic program hosted at the local university. John participated in this program from elementary to middle school. When asked to identify when he became certain that he would attend college, John referenced his involvement in the program:

> INTERVIEWER: When did you become pretty sure that you were going to go to college after high school?
>
> JOHN: I think it was once I started doing all those programs that I felt like I was going to college because it was sort of me thinking that if I'm doing all these and I don't get into college, I would be really disappointed. It was also because I saw myself ready for college because my parents put all of these things, resources into me that I'll be able to go to college and be successful.
>
> INTERVIEWER: Was it a particular moment or was it over this period of time that you felt that?
>
> JOHN: I think it was over this period of time. Because I've always tried my best to be on the top of my classes and then it was also because everyone else kept seeing me as the college-bound student, I started to see myself as that also.

John's participation in the program solidified his desire to attend college. The program itself did not specifically teach about college. Instead, the program was primarily concerned with preparing students to excel in their classes. John, however, connected his participation in the program with college attendance by making sense of why he and his parents put so much effort into preparing him to do well academically. John's decision to pursue higher education was also bolstered by the expectations of the program staff that he was college bound. As a result, John internalized the expectation of college attendance, viewing himself as a hard-working student who would go to college.

A similar process unfolded for Meiying, the daughter of Chinese immigrants. Meiying was the oldest of two children. Neither of her parents had completed college, and both worked in labor-intensive jobs. While she understood that one could still manage to get by even without a college education as her parents had done, it was a path with limited options. College for her came to represent the path that offered her the most opportunities: "Because my parents didn't go to college," she said, "they couldn't do anything. They couldn't do what they want. If I get a good education, I could have more career opportunities. I could make choices I want to make and choose what I want to do. I believe college is the option that would let me have many different choices in the future."

The fact that Meiying needed to rule out the possibility of following in the footsteps of her parents shows that she framed college as one of multiple options for what she might do after high school. While she came to view college as a means to achieve social mobility, it was the academic programs that paved the path for her. Starting in middle school, Meiying participated in multiple academic enrichment programs. Some of these were offered through her school and others through an ethnic Chinese school in her community. These were programs her mother "heard [about] from her friends and the [ethnic] newspaper." In these programs, Meiying learned Mandarin and completed worksheets on academic subjects. As a result of participating in these programs, she decided she would go on to college after high school:

INTERVIEWER: When did you become pretty sure that you were going to go to college?
MEIYING: Middle school.
INTERVIEWER: Tell me what happened then? What led up to that?
MEIYING: I don't know. Since I've been exposed to so many after-school programs, summer programs, academic programs, I feel like after high school it's what I need to do.
INTERVIEWER: Do they tell you that?
MEIYING: I think they kind of expect me to. I think it's just like college after high school that's what I'm expected to do.

Like John, Meiying connected her participation in academic programs to her decision to attend college—these programs immersed her in the expectation that college was the path that she should take. Given how much of her life revolved around academics, it was not difficult for Meiying to imagine a life that involved more schooling, even after she completed high school. While she did not know much about college at that point, her involvement with academic programs enabled her to see college as something for her as well.

Recognition of College as a Potentially Satisfying Experience

John and Meiying both highlighted the expectation of college attendance—when combined with participation in academic programs—as being the motivating factor for enabling them to commit to attending college. However, for most lower-SES students, there were additional elements that helped them arrive at the conclusion that they would attend college. These included needing specific information about college, or even having the opportunity to visit and experience activities on college campuses. For these other students, this necessary information and these experiences came to them during their high school years. In high school, students learned about college admission requirements and life in college, and some even got the opportunity to live on college campuses via summer residential programs at local universities. Through this, they came to learn that college could be a satisfying experience for them, a necessary step in their decision to commit to attending college.

Jack, a Chinese American student, was one such student who required more knowledge about college before fully committing to the idea of college attendance. As someone who had to balance school with household responsibilities, Jack was unsettled about the future. He stated, "I think about a lot of things about my future. I think about a lot of outcomes. I see how these multiple endings could happen now." The different outcomes and multiple endings reflected his understanding of college as one of multiple options, a key part of the framing of college attendance among lower-SES students. Jack further elaborated on these multiple options in his discussion about the aspirations of his friends:

We have [the] same and [also] different ideas. We all want to be successful in a materialistic fashion. All. Maybe not all. Those who plan to go to college want to enjoy it. I have a few friends who don't plan on going to college at all. They plan on not attending college ever and going to work directly or finding some occupation they can be happy with. A friend of mine is excited about going to boot camp for the Navy. I respect that. If he's happy with it, go for it. We all have different goals, but we all want to be happy.

When Jack was a child, his mother introduced him to college as something that he needed to complete. This expectation was not sufficient to convince him to put college in his future plan. He recalled, "I saw college as a concept rather than a campus. It was a concept. High school was when it became real. I learned about it." In high school, college became something he could grasp because he learned more about it:

INTERVIEWER: So when did you become pretty sure of going to college?
JACK: Junior year. Sophomore year was when I wanted to go to college for myself. Junior year is when I decided that I needed to go to college for myself.
INTERVIEWER: Let's talk about sophomore year. What happened?
JACK: AP Bio [Advanced Placement biology]. Again it was just that opportunity to learn and me actually being interested in something for once. I used to go with the flow, motions of school. Go to class, pay attention in class, take notes, do the homework, get good grades, hopefully an A. AP Bio made me want to learn what was happening, pay attention, and take extensive notes. If I didn't still understand, I used to let it pass. But now, I wanted to understand.
INTERVIEWER: So up to this point, you went with the flow but you hit AP Bio and something clicked?
JACK: I was interested in Bio and that helped. It was just the structure of the class that really caught me. I thought that this AP class, if this is like

college, I will like it. I like these kind of more interactive, more critical thinking classes. . . . I felt if college is like this, I want to be there.

Jack's experience in an advanced placement class convinced him that college would be a satisfying experience. Through this class, Jack was able to link the structure and content of a satisfying high school course with the learning that presumably goes on in college classrooms. This connection made college much more tangible. In doing so, the class became a turning point in that it solidified his decision to continue on to college after high school. Whereas previously he was doing well in school for the sake of getting good grades, the experience in this class connected his academic efforts to the end goal of pursuing higher education.

While learning about what college was what motivated students like Jack to become certain of college attendance, other students needed actual experiences on college campuses. These students participated in college preparation programs that took them on college campus visits or put them in summer residential programs on college campuses. These programs helped students who framed college as one of multiple options feel more confident in the idea of attending college. Anthony, an African American student, was one such student. As a kid, he did not know much about college. He remembered, "At first, I thought high school, then that was it. . . . I really wasn't thinking about going to college until high school." By the time he was in high school, his mother had begun taking classes at the nearby university. Yet, despite having a parent who attended college, he still found it difficult to learn about college from her: "I had a lot of questions about how college is. I can't connect with my mom. She had a job and four kids. Her experience is different from my own experience."

Anthony's participation in a college preparation program allowed him to have many of his questions answered, and it gave him the opportunity to spend quality time on a college campus. This experience helped him decide to pursue higher education:

INTERVIEWER: And when did you become pretty sure you were going to go to college after high school?

ANTHONY: After my first summer in UB [the college preparation program]. After that, my mind was made up. I can't get a job after high school. I couldn't do that. That would kill me and stuff.

INTERVIEWER: Something particular happened that summer?

ANTHONY: I lived in the dorms for six weeks without my parents [and] it was a blessing. Walking on campus, it felt good. It wasn't so structured like high school. Go to this class for an hour, go to another class. We would have time between class in college to chill and talk about worldly problems. And it just felt right; this is what I wanted to be at.

Anthony's participation in the summer residential program showed him that college could be a satisfying experience. His knowledge of college up until that point was from watching movies. He recalled learning about college from watching shows that portrayed college as "frat parties, that work was hard, and that it was expensive." By being on campus for six weeks and living the life of a college student, he found the college experience to be enjoyable. This knowledge, combined with his pessimism about being able to acquire a job with just a high school diploma, cemented his decision to pursue higher education. This requirement for additional information and experiences—like the ones that Anthony and Jack highlight—is an example of how the expectation for college, by itself, is often inadequate in convincing lower-SES students to pursue higher education. Lower-SES students need to learn about the college environment or have experiences on a college campus to gradually accept that college is a place that they will enjoy, a necessary condition in their pursuit of higher education.

Linking College Attendance with Social Mobility

Another rationale that lower-SES students drew on to make their decision about going to college was through their recognition that college would provide them with the credentials to move up in society. For example, many students described how their increased knowledge of college informed them that a college degree would open the door to opportunities for upward mobility. Keenly aware of the economic difficulties their family and friends faced due to the lack of a higher education, these students linked college attendance with social mobility. They drew on a comparison between their family experiences and the prospect of a better life with a college degree to make sense of their college attendance decisions. This was the case with Madison, a Laotian American student, who became certain of college attendance due to her participation in a college preparation program that helped her better understand the personal and economic benefits of a college education:

INTERVIEWER: When did you become certain about going to college?

MADISON: Junior year. That's when I started learning about the different systems and options. CT [a college preparation program] would encourage us to think about majors. That's when I started thinking about what I wanted to do in college, and after that I felt like I knew a little bit more than my peers because I was in CT. Because of that, I was a lot more focused.

INTERVIEWER: What did you think about college at this point in junior year?

MADISON: There was a point when I didn't want to go to college. I was like, "College isn't the route for everyone." I was like, "What if it's not the route for me?" I was just really reluctant to go to college. They are just trying to take our money. I could just get a job and start doing things. I thought about it and looked at my family, and thought about how much it would benefit me in the future. And how it would help me broaden my horizon.

Coming from a family and community in which few people have completed college, Madison was understandably hesitant about the prospect of pursuing a higher education degree. She harbored critical preconceptions about college. The fact that she questioned the path of college reflected her frame that college was not the only option, but one of multiple options. For instance, she seriously considered going straight into the labor force after high school. However, she recognized that without a college education, it would be especially difficult to live a comfortable life. Her parents struggled to find work because "they don't have an education." This recognition that she must complete college to avoid the struggles of her family and community paved the way for her to be more accepting of college. The openness toward college enabled her to take advantage of the college preparation program, which exposed her to the structure of higher education and the requirements needed to gain admission. By linking college with economic mobility, Madison was able to rationalize why attending college was something she needed to do.

Marcus, an African American student, explained his rationale (which was similar to Madison's) for attending college. He felt pushed toward college as a result of witnessing how the lack of a higher education made it difficult for his parents to find viable job opportunities. His parents both attended college, but neither had finished. Their family moved around the country multiple times in search of jobs. Even when his father found a good-paying job, his father was subjected to racism. This memory instilled in Marcus the importance of going to college so that he could have more options when faced with racism:

INTERVIEWER: When did you become pretty sure that you were going to go to college after high school?

MARCUS: It was when we lived in Colorado. While we were there, we were making racks, lots of money. My dad, at the time, he was working as a manager at Whole Foods. When he got the job, he was very happy. As time went on, everyone there felt my dad was lower than them because he was Black. He always came home with stuff like that. I knew that I wanted to go to college because, for me, I appreciated my dad for going through all that and accepting everything that they spat at him so he could feed his family.

INTERVIEWER: Having witnessed what your dad went through, you felt college would allow you to avoid that?

MARCUS: Not necessarily help me avoid it. I knew that if I was on the job, it could happen anywhere, whether I go to college or not. The main thing that I thought about was that if I'm making all that money, if I choose to quit a job, I can quit and get a new one. My dad, he didn't have that opportunity.

Marcus recognized his father's path as a possibility; his father was able to make good money from a job without a college education. This experience and understanding shaped his frame of college as one of multiple options. However, the lack of an education limited opportunities for his father when confronted with a distressing racist work environment. As a result, Marcus came to see college as the path that would help him deal with racism in the workplace. Marcus did not view a college education as something that would shelter him from racism. He acknowledged that he could be the target of racism anytime and anywhere. However, he believed a college degree would provide him with more opportunities for good-paying jobs so that he could move on from racist workplaces.

Maria, a Mexican American student, also linked going to college with improved job prospects, a connection that convinced her of the importance of a college degree. She lived with her mother, who was employed at a shopping center. Here, she talked about how she came to the conclusion that she would go on to college:

INTERVIEWER: So when did you become very sure that you were going to go to college after high school?

MARIA: At the end of my freshman year, I was like, "I'm going to college no matter what." I'm in high school, I can't just work, that's boring. I don't want to do that. I don't want to just work. I don't want to be in the labor force doing extra work that I don't need to be doing to earn a salary or wages that I can't even sustain myself with.

INTERVIEWER: Do you remember what happened freshman year that got you to be like that?

MARIA: So, when I was a freshman my boyfriend was a senior. . . . He graduated when he barely turned 17. And I saw him graduate but then after he just worked so I was like I don't want to do that. . . . But I think the main thing was just seeing him not going to college was like, "What are you doing with your life?" I mean, I'm not going to leave you because you didn't go to college, but I don't want to do that. I think that was the main thing for me.

Maria recognized the difficulties of finding good-paying jobs without a college degree from observations of the labor market experiences of her mother and boyfriend. To avoid this difficulty, Maria eliminated the potential path of working immediately right after high school, a reflection of her frame of college as one of multiple options. Like other lower-SES students who drew on a social mobility rationale to justify their decision to pursue higher education, Maria expressed optimism at her ability to find better paying jobs with a college degree. It was this comparative evaluation grounded in her observations of the economic struggles of her family and friends and the prospect of a college degree for economic mobility that solidified Maria's desire to pursue higher education.

Evaluation of College Admission Requirements

Another important way in which lower-SES students became certain about college attendance was by assessing whether their credentials would be sufficient to get them into college. These students were interested in college but they were unsure if they could get into college. As such, college occupied a tentative position in their future until they became confident that they had the credentials to be admitted into college. This confidence emerged through learning about college requirements and finding that they met these criteria. In doing so, these students engaged in a process of academic evaluation in which they compared their academic credentials to the admission requirements of colleges. Carlos, a Mexican American student, was one of the students who needed confirmation that he had the requisite academic credentials to get into college. He lived with his father, a construction worker, and two brothers. Seeing the physical toll that construction work exacted on his father made Carlos focus on doing well in his classes. Despite this focus on working hard in school, it was not until his later years of high school that he became certain of college attendance:

INTERVIEWER: When did you become pretty sure that you were actually going to go to college?

CARLOS: I was pretty sure during my junior year. They've always said that as a sophomore, your junior year is the most important year because it's the year that they actually look at for college. After I ended junior year, I had good grades. I was like I could make it and I just need to finish this last semester of my junior year. Now I am here, about to finish my last semester of high school, I'm college bound.

In the absence of a family member who could guide him through the college process, Carlos had to wait until high school to figure out what he needed to do to get into college. Once he figured this out and realized that he met the criteria, college attendance became a real possibility.

For a few students for whom this rationale remained a key part of their decision-making process, it was through the act of applying or of receiving acceptance letters that college attendance became real for them. Natalie, a Chinese American student, is one such student. She lived with her mother, who worked as a cashier at a local shop, and she attended what was considered the top public school in the city. She was tentative about college given her family background:

INTERVIEWER: When did you become certain about going to college?

NATALIE: I was always skeptical that I would get into college. Everyone made it seem like it's something that you probably can't reach. What really hit me that I was going to go to college was that moment when I hit the I accept button to [UC] Davis and I was like, "I am going to college." I knew I had to finish high school first but I knew I was going to graduate. So that really hit me. This summer I'm like, "I'm going to college, oh my god!"

INTERVIEWER: You said it sounded so far-fetched, tell me more about that? What were people saying?

NATALIE: You see these American dreams and quotes and you only see these middle-class kids going to college. You don't see kids in the slums going to college. They don't advertise that. Being low income, my mom didn't go to college. She dropped out, and it just makes it seem so much farther than it actually is.

For Natalie, her understanding of college attendance was influenced by an awareness that she was low income and that she attended a high school in which upperclassmen have encountered difficulties in trying to get into the colleges of their choice. She recognized that the image of someone going to college did not reflect people like her who were from low-income backgrounds. Given that she attended a competitive high school and students were aiming to get into top colleges, she linked getting into college with getting into a top college. This understanding of college exerted even more pressure on her, and thus she was unsure of her ability to make it to college. It was only when she accepted her spot at a nearby university that she became certain that she would become a college student.

Lower-SES students' uncertainty about getting into college contributed to their frame of college as one of multiple options. These students wanted to go to college, but having grown up in an environment in which few people had gone on to college, they harbored doubts about their ability to gain admission into college. Unlike their higher-SES counterparts who framed college as inevitable and had no doubts about getting into college, lower-SES students needed information about college admission requirements and, for some students, acceptance letters to believe that college was a real possibility.

Internalization of Expectations from Families and Peers

Although not as common, there were several lower-SES students who took for granted the idea of college attendance from a very young age. These few lower-SES students drew on a rationale that resembled that of their higher-SES counterparts—they knew from a young age that they would have to go through college. The lower-SES students who fell into this category lacked the frame of college attendance as one out of multiple options that most of their lower-SES peers had. They were unable to pinpoint a moment or time when they consciously decided that they would attend college; instead, they knew for as long as they could remember that they would continue to college after high school. The expectations of their parents and their community were sufficient for them to internalize the idea of college attendance. Of the students interviewed, it was primarily Asian American students that fell into this category. Lily, a Vietnamese American student, was one such student. Her father worked as a clock assembler, and her mother was unemployed. When asked about when she decided she would attend college on completion of high school, she responded:

> It was always there in the back of my head. I never had a moment where I never thought I wouldn't go to college. It was always expected in my family. My dad is big on education. He himself was immersed in going to school and college even though he didn't go to college. He enlisted in the army for the Vietnam War. He instead encourages his kids to do that in place of him, to live the life he didn't get to live. The only two kids he has that would be able to do that are my sister and me. My sister is done with her BA [bachelor's degree]. With me, I plan to do exactly what he expects.

Lily had a frame of college attendance as inevitable. Her parents knew of college, but almost nothing about college life or the process of applying to college. Yet, despite learning little about college from her parents, Lily knew from a young age that she wanted to attend college. In reflecting on her earliest recollections of college, she fondly remembered developing an interest in becoming a doctor in third grade via an afterschool program. Later on, her father bought her a stethoscope to play with at home. Through a discussion with her parents about becoming a doctor, she linked her career interest with attending college.

Shawn, a Chinese American, is another student who took for granted the idea of college attendance. To explain his frame of college attendance, Shawn referenced the expectation of college attendance present in his social environment. Shawn lived with his grandmother and mother. He did not realize that his family received government assistance in the form of food stamps until he applied for financial aid to go to college. This was due to the fact that his mother wanted to be protective of him regarding their family hardships. Shawn said, "She did a lot of things to shield me from the harsh reality of life." Nevertheless, like Lily, because of specific actions by his family, alongside expectations of his student peers, Shawn internalized the idea that he was going to college, something that he said left him pretty sure of his eventual college attendance from as far back as he could remember:

> INTERVIEWER: When did you become pretty sure that you were going to go to college after high school?
>
> SHAWN: I always knew I was going to college.
>
> INTERVIEWER: Tell me more.
>
> SHAWN: I was on this narrow-minded path since I was a kid, I'm going to a college. I didn't know what a college was. That's pretty much the standard route for me, for Asians. You are going to go to middle school, high school, college and then get a job.

Shawn expressed an understanding of college as just another step in the process of schooling that he must go through before entering the workforce. Whereas other lower-SES students took their social class background into account in trying to make sense of college attendance, Shawn felt he was just like any other kid at his socioeconomically diverse public school. His social class background was not an important part of his identity because his mother had largely concealed it. As a result, his identity as Asian American was what was most visible to him. He internalized the stereotype of Asian Americans as high achieving, believing that he would pursue higher education just like any other Asian American student. Though they are lower-SES, these students had a frame of college as inevitable and just another step in their schooling.

College as Inevitable

Unlike most lower SES-students, higher-SES students consistently framed college attendance as something that was inevitable. College for them represented merely another step in their educational journey. This frame of college attendance among higher-SES students was evident in their responses to the specific question of when they became certain that they would attend college. They directly stated that they always knew college was the next step after high school and that they did not entertain any thoughts of not going to college. Many initially expressed bewilderment at the question because pursuing higher education represented the default option. Rarely did these students talk about being encouraged to go to college. Their families and communities assumed they would go to college. And these students themselves internalized this implicit expectation. In doing so, higher-SES students framed college attendance as inevitable and a natural progression of their schooling. Students made sense of this frame of college attendance by referencing the college-going culture of their family and community. When higher-SES students drew on rationales to make sense of their college trajectory, it was primarily to validate their taken-for-granted attitude toward college attendance.

In what follows, I organize the responses of higher-SES students based on how students made sense of their frame of college attendance, specifically whether they attributed it to their families or the larger social context of their communities. I place special emphasis on highlighting the elements in their frame of college attendance and, when applicable, the rationales they bring up to make sense of their frame.

Internalization of Expectations from Families

Many higher-SES students brought up family socialization to make sense of their frame toward college attendance. For instance, students like Yuna assumed they would attend college because it was what members of their family had done. Yuna, a Japanese American student, was born in the United States but grew up in Japan with her parents and older sister. At the beginning of high school, she left Japan to live with her aunt in the Bay Area to continue her schooling. Both of her parents are college graduates. Her family environment shaped how she thought about her college attendance:

INTERVIEWER: So when did you become certain you were going to college?

YUNA: I always knew I was going to go to college. I don't think I even thought about not going to college. But recently I heard a lot of stories about people who are taking a year off to do volunteer work or travel or something. That sounds like so much fun. But I don't think I can do that because I don't know what I want to do to make up for that time.

INTERVIEWER: That's so interesting, you never thought about not going to college?

YUNA: Because I think it's a family thing. It's parents urging their children to go to a college, and it seems like a crazy idea not to. You don't know what you are doing with your life. So I feel like since I was born, it was already expected that I go to a college.

INTERVIEWER: Can you remember things when you were younger that pushed you to go to college?

YUNA: Since my sister went to college, I guess. It seems like a faraway thing but it seems like something I was going to have to do. I knew I was going to go to college.

By discussing college attendance as something that she always knew would happen, Yuna framed college attendance as inevitable. Despite not knowing much about college at a young age, she knew it was something that she herself would have to experience because that was what her parents and sibling had done. Given her family history, Yuna could not imagine another alternative beyond matriculating to college. Yuna's reasoning for her attitude toward college attendance drew upon her family history and the understanding that going to college was what a normal person in her circumstance would do.

The case of Macy, a white student, demonstrates how early family exposure to college as a positive social experience shaped students' frame of college attendance. Both of Macy's parents hold advanced degrees in their respective fields. As a child, Macy visited colleges with her parents and met their college friends. She recalled hearing her parents and their college friends talking warmly about their experiences while in college. Macy drew on this experience to make sense of why she always assumed that she would attend college:

INTERVIEWER: When did you become certain about going to college? That after high school college is next?

MACY: I think that has always been the case. Just because it's always been the case.

INTERVIEWER: As a kid?

MACY: First time I went to Boston College when I was a lot younger and my dad was like, "I went to college here." I'm sure if one of us [children] expressed interest in not going to college, my parents would want to have a dialogue about it just to try to figure it out. That's never been the case. It's something that we have always wanted to do.

INTERVIEWER: Why do you think that's the case?

MACY: I don't know. I guess it's word of mouth. Our parents got really good experiences and have lifelong friends who have visited us and are like, "This is my best friend from college. We always have all these great memories," and they would tell us all these stories that were very fun like, "We work very hard. Hard work paid off. We work at a job that we are excited to work for every day." I guess we all understand that in today's world it's hard to be successful without having a college degree. . . . Not going to college is not something that we talk about. Both my sister and brother, we have always wanted to go to college. It sounds very fun. It's a very great experience so we haven't really discussed that.

For as long as Macy could remember, she knew she would be attending college. She pointed out that pursuing higher education was something that she wanted for herself, indicating that college was not necessarily pushed on her. College attendance was not imposed on Macy because there was little doubt in the minds of her parents that she would attend college. As a result, there was no need for Macy's parents to convince her that college was the right path for her. Instead, by exposing Macy early on to happy memories of their college experiences, Macy's parents facilitated her internalization of the implicit expectation of college attendance.

Jaime, a white student, understood college as just a continuation of her educational trajectory. Both of her parents are college graduates, and she also had an older sister that was in college:

INTERVIEWER: When did you became certain that you were going to attend college?

JAIME: It never really was a doubt. It was something that was expected.

INTERVIEWER: Interesting. Tell me more? What happened? What made you feel like that?

JAIME: Both my parents went to college. Our whole family has gone to college. Pretty much everyone in [our community] goes to college. It's seen as the next step. My parents have been saving money so that I can go to college my whole life. It's just seen as the next thing that I am going to do.

INTERVIEWER: What did you know about college growing up?

JAIME: I knew it was something you do after high school and something expected of me and my peers. It was seen as another step. Other than that I don't know. It wasn't something that ever stressed me growing up. I didn't know too much about it. I think just knowing that it's another school you go to, and it's a lot harder, and another step.

In an environment in which her family and many in the community had attended college, Jaime came to expect the same for herself. Even with little knowledge about college as a young child, Jaime was very confident that she would attend college. Jaime brought up an important element in the frame of college attendance, which is that college is merely another step in the educational process. The completion of high school did not entail contemplation about what path one should take; instead, it merely signified the beginning of another level of education. The inevitability of college attendance for Jaime was further supported by the fact that her parents had already set aside a fund for her college expenses.

For Nick, a white student, college represented not just the continuation of his schooling but the first of multiple steps in his post–high school educational journey. Nick's parents both hold graduate degrees in their respective fields. In answering a question about his parents' expectations, he revealed how he framed college attendance: "Both my parents want me to go to college. I think that was always an assumption rather than 'we hope you go to college.' It was, 'You will be going to college.' Not in a pretentious way, but it's expected. My mom definitely said, 'When you go to graduate school, whenever you do.' It depends on what I do. Maybe I have a new interest in college that won't translate into higher education after undergrad. I think whatever I do, they are going to support me."

Nick's experience is an example of how parents of higher-SES students engage with their children about the future that reflects an implicit expectation of college attendance. Nick and his parents did not talk openly about college attendance because they assumed that Nick would pursue higher education. The idea that Nick would attend college is viewed as a foregone conclusion such that his mother had already broached the topic of graduate school with him.

Lewis, a Chinese American student, actually considered other options besides college immediately after high school. While options such as going into the military and taking a gap year were considered, they were not necessarily alternatives to college. Rather, they represented stepping-stones to college that could mitigate some of the financial costs of higher education (military option) or enhance the college experience itself (gap year option):

INTERVIEWER: When did you know for sure you were going to college?

LEWIS: I think it was impressed upon me by my mom. I even asked her about taking a gap year. She was like, "As long as you could find something to do." I'm more keen on going to college. I'm not sure. I'm going through a lot of thoughts. College seems to be the most stable option. I haven't done research on other alternative options. Enlisting in the military for two years crossed my mind. They do give you a generous G.I. Bill so that is good but I could also die. I do know two people who did a fifth year of high school as a gap year in Europe. One of my friends went to Finland and another went to Germany to work on their language skills. My language is Chinese and I'm not too keen on going to China.

Lewis attributed his frame of college as inevitable to his mother, who "impressed upon" him the necessity of college attendance. As a result, he knew and assumed from a young age that he had to go to college. While he could delay college in pursuit of opportunities that can improve his college experiences, college still assumed a near certain prospect in his future.

Together, the examples of higher-SES students in this section point to how parents and older siblings created an environment that enabled these students to accept college as an impending reality for them. Rarely did these students point to the need for information or experiences, like that of their lower-SES peers, to rationalize their decision about college attendance. Higher-SES students' assumptions that they would pursue higher education did not require them to rationalize why college was the right choice for them. In the rare case that a rationale was brought up, as in the case of Macy who cited social satisfaction with college life, it represented her efforts to understand her own frame of reference of college as inevitable rather than to justify why she chose college over the alternative options. The behaviors and experiences of their parents and siblings were sufficient motivations for them to assume college was the right path for them.

The Impact of Community Influences

In addition to the significant role of family socialization in the way higher SES-students framed college attendance, other students noted that, on top of this family influence, the larger social context of their communities also had an important influence. This latter group of students referenced the pervasive but unspoken expectation of college attendance that followed them throughout their lives in multiple social spaces. Anna, a white student, was one such student. Her parents are immigrants from Europe, and both hold graduate degrees. She grew up in a very competitive academic environment in which almost every student continued on to college. Given this environment, it was not surprising that she talked about the social environment when asked about college attendance:

INTERVIEWER: When did you become certain about attending college after high school?

ANNA: I've always known that I wanted to go to a four-year college. It's always something my parents talk about because why not. It's shown up in conversations. I spend a lot of time on the internet basically my entire life and a lot of colleges show up. I remembered being six or seven [years old], we have to fill out a survey. "What do you want to do after you graduate from high school?" And I was like four-year college for sure. No matter what, I'm going to a four-year college. The environment that I grew up in, which is not good for everyone, but for me it was highly beneficial. I'd always known that it was happening.

INTERVIEWER: You say the environment expects you to go to college. Tell me more about that.

ANNA: Basically, college preparedness was the primary goal of a lot of my educators from kindergarten up. It always seems like something that was inevitable. Everyone was like, "Go to college because why wouldn't you? That's how you get a job, get a good job, that your children are fed." I think I'm so desensitized to that because I've been around people who go to college my entire life.

Anna always knew that she would attend college, a reflection of her frame of college attendance as inevitable. This understanding of higher education came about through interactions in multiple spaces from her family to the internet to schools that reinforced the notion of college attendance as an accepted fact. In such an environment, anyone who entertained other ideas besides college was viewed with disapproval. To make sense of her frame of college attendance, Anna drew on a social mobility rationale that linked college attendance with economic success in life.

Emily, a Chinese American student and the daughter of two college graduates, also pointed to the role of social forces outside the family when discussing when she became certain that she would attend college. Like other students, she framed college attendance as inevitable, but she drew on a slightly different rationale to make sense of her understanding of college:

INTERVIEWER: Tell me about when you became certain that you will attend college?

EMILY: I always expected to go to college. I knew that I would probably go to college and go through what everyone else was doing. Apply to college because there's a stigma against not going to college. I thought I'm going to apply to college and major in business which is something I don't want to do. It came up that there was something I was looking forward to in college, a job or profession in my thirties and forties. It kind of made me active and more motivated to go to school and college. I mean I was always going to go there anyway.

INTERVIEWER: Tell me more about that—that you were always going to college. People around you doing that or your parents telling you that?

EMILY: I think most people in America think that if you really want to succeed in life, you should go to college. It's a big stepping-stone. It's a necessary path to earn a high-paying job usually. So yeah, I've had that feeling. Plus, I've worked so hard. I think one of the reasons we are taught to pursue college is because it's been ingrained in me to work hard so I can get in to college.

For Emily, who grew up surrounded by many people who had gone to college, college attendance represented what people do to become successful. In this environment, individuals who did not pursue higher education were frowned upon. Emily, like other higher-SES students, took for granted that she would attend college. As a result, there was no need for encouragements or motivations to push her to attend college. By invoking the stigma attached to those who did not attend college, Emily was simply drawing on a social mobility rationale to justify her taken-for-granted attitude toward college attendance.

Conclusion

Social class background represents one of the key contexts that shapes how students decide to attend college (Biggart and Furlong 1996; Beattie 2002; Grodsky and Jones 2007; Kim 2012). The decision making of students from disadvantaged backgrounds is often viewed through a rational choice lens, in which students are depicted as making a deliberate decision to pursue higher education. In contrast, advantaged students from middle- and upper-middle-class families are portrayed as automatically attending college with little to no deliberation about their decision (Horvat 2001; Grodsky and Jackson 2009; Grodsky and Riegle-Crumb 2010).

As this chapter shows, however, the nature and process of the college attendance decision making is linked to the meaning students attached to higher education. Drawing on the concept of frames, it is possible to see how higher-SES students framed college attendance as inevitable and a natural progression of schooling. By framing college attendance as such, higher-SES students assumed that they would get into college and that college was merely another step in their educational journey. In contrast, most lower-SES students framed college attendance as one of multiple options after high school. The end of high school represented a key transitional point for lower-SES in that they must decide to continue on with their education or pursue another path. Given the uncertainty surrounding college attendance, lower-SES students needed to convince themselves and sometimes those around them that college was the right path for them. The decision to attend college for most lower-SES students was a process that unfolded over time during middle and high school as students accumulated knowledge about college and experiences on college campuses.

While social class influenced the frames of higher education, all students made sense of their decision to attend college based on overlapping rationales, particularly those that linked college attendance with social mobility and social satisfaction. This shows that there was a consensus among students from different social class backgrounds about why individuals should pursue higher education. However, whereas higher-SES students drew on the rationales to validate their taken-for-granted stance toward college attendance, lower-SES students used the rationales to justify why college attendance rather than another path was right for them. Moreover, while students referenced overlapping types of rationales, the content of these rationales differed across social class. Higher-SES students drew on rationales that reflected what sociologist Roslyn Mickelson (1990) refers to as a set of abstract attitudes, general views or understandings about the importance of higher education. In contrast, lower-SES students brought up rationales that reflected concrete attitudes rooted in real-life experiences and observations of their family and communities.

This abstract attitude versus concrete attitude distinction was most readily observed in the social mobility and college satisfaction rationales that students drew on. In the social mobility rationale, higher-SES students spoke generally about the necessity of a college degree for success. In contrast, lower-SES students referenced observations of family and friends struggling to make ends meet as factors that pushed them to see college as the way to avoid a similar predicament. For the college satisfaction rationale, higher-SES students discussed the positive experiences of their family members, and they expected to have a similar experience in college. Lower-SES students, on the other hand, spoke about actual experiences, such as visiting a college or living on a college campus. The content expressed in the rationales showed that in their pursuit of higher education, higher-SES students sought to replicate the experiences of their college-educated parents, whereas lower-SES students tried to avoid the predicaments of their non-college-educated family and friends.

The road to college enrollment was one fraught with uncertainties and potential derailment for lower-SES students. Even among the pool of high-achieving, lower-SES students in this study, as this chapter shows, individuals still needed frequent affirmations that college was the right place for them. As their rationales demonstrated, these affirmations can take many forms. Early on in their schooling, lower-SES students benefited from teachers and college preparation program staff who told them they had what it took to go to college. Later on, students needed to know what college was like in the form of exposure to colleges and even experiences on college campuses. Lower-SES students had to become convinced not only that they could make it into college, but that college would be worth the effort and that it would be a satisfying experience.

While most lower-SES students became certain of college attendance later on in their middle and high school years, the students' ethnic or racial group also appeared to affect when they reached the conclusion that college was right for them. Asian American students, for example, were more likely than their African American and Hispanic peers to know about the concept of college at a much younger age. Though they knew little about college as children and were uncertain about college in their future, Asian American students knew it was some type of schooling. As young children in elementary school, Asian American students were introduced to the concept of college by their parents, their academic programs, or older siblings. Asian American parents, particularly Chinese and Vietnamese parents, learned about college through the ethnic media or their social networks with other parents, including relatives. They tried to impress upon their children the notion of college as something that students needed to pursue. Some parents put their children into afterschool or summer academic programs or enrolled them in ethnic schools to facilitate their children's journey to college.

Hispanic and African American students were more likely to be exposed to the notion of college at a much later point than their lower-SES Asian American peers. Anthony, an African American student discussed in this chapter, noted that, as a child, he assumed his education ended on the completion of high school. It was not until he got to high school that he learned about college as another level of education beyond high school. Martina, a Mexican American student, learned about college early on in high school when she saw her brother attend community college. However, the brother's community college experience was not as relevant and useful for her own journey because she was intent on a four-year college. This was in contrast to the Asian American students who had older siblings or relatives who had attended or completed degrees at four-year universities. The experiences of these older siblings and relatives were very helpful for these Asian American students as they navigated high school.

In this chapter, it becomes increasingly clear how the experiences and knowledge rooted in a family's social class background structures students' college choice decision-making process. Though both groups of students are high achieving, they each came to the decision about going to college from vastly different points of departure. The frames students have about college attendance and the points at which they became certain of college attendance have implications for how students prepare for college and the types of colleges they consider, the other aspects of the college choice decision-making process in this research. When and how students learned about college, reflected in their frame of college attendance, also shapes what colleges they think are appropriate for them.

2

Frames of College Preparation

● ● ● ● ● ● ● ● ● ● ● ● ● ● ● ● ● ● ● ●

Maria is a Mexican American high school student from a family in a lower socioeconomic class. She described two specific things that she believed would put her in the best position for getting into college: doing well in her courses, and becoming involved with activities beyond the classroom. She stated that she wanted her résumé for college to show that she "could go above and beyond being a good student." Satisfying the first part of her strategy came relatively easily; she took the most rigorous courses available at her school. The second part, however, required more intentionality and initiative. She sought out opportunities to give back to the community and her high school. For instance, she actively solicited support for a ballot measure that would bring new funding to the schools in her city. She was recognized for her effort with a scholarship. One summer, she participated in a medical internship at a nearby prestigious private university. Another summer, she took part in a summer legal fellowship program where she was placed with the investigation unit at the city's police department.

Anna, a white student with a higher socioeconomic status (SES), pursued a similar strategy. She took as many advanced placement (AP) courses as possible. Driven by the desire to do "a lot of things outside the box," she participated in a coding competition in which she and her team of female participants won the top award for designing a test preparation application. She also founded a new club at her school and headed up multiple other clubs that included speech and debate, the school's chamber music, the book club, and an environmental club. Outside school, she interned for the Sierra Club, a national environmental nonprofit organization, and the United States Department of Agriculture.

On the surface, it looks like both Maria and Anna did similar things to prepare for college, but on further analysis, there is a subtle but significant difference in their understanding or framing of what college preparation entailed. As part of her strategy, Maria sought to do things that would convey to colleges that she was someone who was strong in academics and involved with extracurricular activities outside the classroom. Maria's strategy reflected her frame of college preparation as doing what was necessary to demonstrate that she was a well-rounded student. Her quote about going beyond just "being a good student" reflected this frame of college preparation as projecting an identity of a well-rounded student.

In contrast, Anna framed college preparation as pursuing opportunities that would distinguish herself from the rest of her peers. Her quote about doing things outside the box reflected this frame. Whereas being a well-rounded student meant focusing on accumulating extracurricular activities to demonstrate students' engagement beyond the classroom, distinguishing oneself from others emphasized the uniqueness or special features of their academic and extracurricular records. In doing so, Maria and Anna framed their preparation for college in ways that reflected the experiences, understandings, and expectations of other students from their social class backgrounds.

This chapter analyzes the preparation approaches of students and the various types of activities students participated in as they readied themselves for college. Like Maria and Anna, all students understood that doing well in the most rigorous courses available in their high schools was essential to gaining admission into colleges, especially their top choices. They also recognized that grades by themselves were inadequate and that they needed to do more. Thus students became involved in academic activities and other extracurricular activities to enhance their credentials for college admission.

The strategies employed by students and the types of activities they participated in reflected students' social class backgrounds and their framing of what college preparation entailed. Lower-SES students framed college preparation as projecting an identity of a well-rounded student, which consisted of cultivating social and academic skills necessary to succeed in college and participating in extra-curricular activities. In contrast, the approach of higher-SES students was driven by the desire to stand out among their peers. This framing of college preparation led higher-SES students to seek out activities that they believed distinguished themselves from others. This strategy centered as much on the activities they engaged in as it did on how they rationalized their involvement. In discussing their approach and involvement, higher-SES students frequently emphasized how they were unique from others in what they did or in how they did it—their involvement was framed as a reflection of their individual passion and personal autonomy.

Fitting In: Developing Competence and Projecting Well-Roundedness

The preparation approach of most lower-SES students was aimed at acquiring the skills needed to succeed in college and at projecting to colleges that they were well-rounded students who have interests and commitments beyond just doing well in the classroom. In other words, lower-SES students were working hard to fit the typical profile of college students. They wanted to establish for themselves and for others that they were like other college-bound students: capable and involved. Aware of the lower quality of education they received in their schools, many lower-SES students were intent on proving that they also belonged in college.

Developing Competence: Academic Knowledge and Skills

When reflecting on their approaches to preparing for college, lower-SES students stressed the need to develop the various social and academic skill sets that would enable them to thrive in college. They were genuinely invested in making sure that they were prepared to face the challenges of a new and different academic environment. One path they believed would help them to develop academic competence was taking AP Courses. Carlos, a Mexican American student, articulated the importance of coursework and the development of skills in his preparation for college:

> I guess the only way that I prepared was by taking advantage of AP classes. They say AP classes, they resemble college and stuff like that. I feel like I just use AP classes to get myself ahead of everybody. Also, when I was in middle school, I didn't show a lot of emotions. I wasn't outgoing and stuff. High school prepared me for college because if you want to have a good time, you want to have relationships with people you've never talked to, make friends and be social and outgoing. I prepared myself for that in high school because you have to be social in college and that's what I did. That's how I prepared for college.

Carlos saw high school as a site for developing the academic and social competence for college success. He linked the structure and rigor of AP classes to college courses. Taking AP classes represented a path toward moving ahead of other students and preparing him for the rigor of college courses. Recognizing that success in college was also about one's ability to connect with others, Carlos became intentional about developing his social skills during high school.

Doing well in classes could only do so much to prepare lower-SES students. Lower-SES students were well aware that they attended high schools with limited resources. This meant that they could not just depend on their high schools to adequately prepare them for college. Sofia, a Mexican American student, discussed how she learned from her older sister (who was a college student at the time) that the preparation she was getting from her high school was not going to be enough:

INTERVIEWER: How did you prepare for college?

SOFIA: I always thought about getting As. I just thought about the grades, and not [necessarily about] learning. It wasn't until high school that I realized that I wasn't learning as much. In high school, I learned about the A-G [high school course requirements for college] requirements to have a competitive application to go to college.

INTERVIEWER: When did you realize it wasn't just getting good grades, but you also had to learn in your classes?

SOFIA: In class, I would just sit and do worksheets. When I was at R. High School, I would be like, "I'm not learning much. How am I going to go to higher education if I don't even know the basics." I felt like I wasn't prepared. That's when my sister told me she went through the same thing, and her transition to college was very difficult.

The recognition that their high schools were limited in what they could do to prepare students for success in college made lower-SES students less dependent on their high school. Sofia's awareness of her school's history of inadequate preparation of college-bound students reflected her doubts about her ability to flourish in college. These worries were shared by other students as well. While common among lower-SES students, such fears were nonexistent among higher-SES students. Another example of this can be seen in the way Andrea, a Chinese American student, joined an academic program to supplement her preparation for college:

I joined CT [a college preparation program] and they recruit in 8th grade. You fill out a form and then you have to do a summer session. I mostly joined because I knew they would give me tutoring help because I knew I would eventually take Calculus. In the first year, they make you take a certain amount of classes. It's like an hour or so of tutoring or extracurricular stuff or academic things and then there's college affairs. I started strong freshmen year and then sophomore year, I didn't have any AP classes so I went less than I should have. Junior year, I had four to five AP classes, and then I started to go again.

The comments of Carlos, Andrea, and Sofia demonstrate one aspect of lower-SES students' frame of college preparation. This aspect concerned how they understand what it means to be academically qualified to be a college student. To prove to themselves and to colleges that they were competent students, these students not only took as many rigorous courses as possible but they also made sure that they were learning in those courses. When the learning did not match what they expected was required of them in college, they sought resources outside the classroom to bolster their preparedness for college.

In addition to classes, another way that lower-SES students sought to demonstrate their competence was through their performance on the standardized tests, specifically the ACT and SAT. Students understood the importance of these scores in how they would be evaluated by colleges, and they took advantage of opportunities to prepare for these exams. Most lower-SES students were able to get access to some type of test preparation instruction via their participation in academic programs. The quality of the instruction varied, from an adult working with students intermittently to a structured, week-by-week instructional program. At one end of the spectrum was the preparation experience of Carlos. His high school offered a college preparation program that sought to make college a reality for low-income students. He described the assistance he received in preparing for the standardized aptitude tests: "The program director helped us out. She would spend like some days after school of her time to teach us things before we get there. That was just the SAT. The ACT I didn't really get much help. It was just based on what I knew. Most of the SAT, I prepared by using everything I learned from math and English classes. I didn't really prepare myself enough because coming from a low-income school, you really don't have the resources for you to get help. It is kind of hard."

In the case of Carlos, the assistance would be best described as a college-educated adult troubleshooting with students as they came across challenging questions. On the other end of the spectrum was the experience of Martina, a Mexican American student, who participated in two test preparation programs, one provided by her high school and the other her academic program:

INTERVIEWER: What kind of support did you get from your school in preparing for college?

MARTINA: They offered us SAT prep classes that were also afterschool for 2 hours. That was about it.

INTERVIEWER: What did you think of these classes?

MARTINA: I actually liked them because it was a different program that came in to give us the classes. I felt like I was understanding more of the questions they were asking. We took practice SATs and I kind of got more into how I needed to better my scores and stuff like that.

While the experiences of Carlos and Martina reflect opposite ends of the spectrum of the quality of instruction, most students experienced something in between, receiving some type of methodical instruction from one source, typically their college preparation program. Some students supplemented the instruction with their own preparation. Katherine, a Vietnamese American student, procured test materials to study during her own time:

INTERVIEWER: How did you prepare for standardized tests?

KATHERINE: Through UB [a college preparation program], they have SAT test preparation in the classes in the summer. That's one way I prepared. On top of that, I got workbooks and I would look through them. I used the flash cards from the SAT and I also bought an ACT book to familiarize myself with the concepts. That's how I prepared myself. There are also essay-writing drills in my UB classes. There are time limits and we have to try very hard to get everything down. I got the hint of it. I write down my opinion on the topic and then I move on.

Lower-SES students like Carlos, Martina, and Katherine recognized the importance of doing well on the aptitude tests as a way to demonstrate their academic competence, and they took it upon themselves to seek out institutional resources and other ways to prepare for these tests. This was on top of taking a rigorous course load that included as many honors or AP classes as were available at their high schools. Lower-SES students were not just merely interested in signaling to colleges that they were qualified. They genuinely tried to accumulate the skills and knowledge that they believed would enable them to adapt and succeed in college.

Developing Competence: Behavioral Skills and Habits

Similar to the previous group of lower-SES students who felt that they needed more academic development outside their courses, other lower-SES students emphasized the importance of needing to know what goes on during college so that they could develop the behavioral skills necessary to adapt to the new challenges. The emphasis on behavioral skills, in addition to the previously mentioned academic knowledge, constituted a major component of lower-SES students' frame of college preparation as developing the competence to succeed in college. To develop these behavioral skills, the best preparation was to actually experience college—or a simulation of it. The opportunity to participate in summer residential programs on college campuses was immensely pivotal in helping lower-SES students prepare for the routines of college. For most students, their participation in the residential programs was their first time away from home for an extended time, the first opportunity to live independently away from their family. Students got the chance to experience the routines of college life from living in the dorms to taking classes and interacting with professors. Jay, a Chinese American student, reflected on his approach of using the summer residential program to mentally prepare him for college:

> I made sure I went to the summer residential program with UB because it gave me the experiences of how college would feel, like waking up in the morning, study hours, office hours, study hall. Stuff like that. They gave us a good way of balancing our time. It also gave us opportunity. I actually spent the summer at UC Berkeley so it gave me a good idea of what UC Berkeley was like. It gave me opportunities to talk with professors that actually taught at UC Berkeley, [talk with] kids who go to UC Berkeley. That gave me an insight about what college life is like. I felt like a freshman in college. That helped me out a lot.

The summer programs were not simply about the structure and routines of college. They were also about exposure to the different life experiences that diverse college student communities bring with them. Living in a new environment meant that students had to learn to adapt. As such, lower-SES students viewed these opportunities as valuable insights into what it meant to be a typical college student. These types of engagements and experiences were part of their framing of college preparation, which required them to learn as much about college as possible. For Marcus, an African American student, his experiences in the summer programs taught him that he could no longer depend on his family if he encountered an unfamiliar situation; he had to make the best decision for himself as part of the process of living independently in a college environment:

> MARCUS: UB, specifically the six-week program over the summer. That really helped me get insight when I get to college, what I will be doing. We only took two classes, but it was meant to be the full college experience. It's like what you are going to do in college. That's one of the things that they help me prepare.
>
> INTERVIEWER: How was the six-week college program?
>
> MARCUS: It was interesting. That was the first time I ever left home for a long extended period of time by myself, not depending on anyone else. Usually, if I'm not sure about anything I go to my parents and older brothers and ask them for advice. This experience, I had to make decisions based on past decisions and based on what I thought was right.

The summer residential experiences informed students of the differences between high school and college. Students frequently referenced how the programs prepared them for college by introducing them to the routines of a college student and helping them identify the skills they needed to develop so they would thrive in college. These new routines required students to adapt and acquire new habits. Time management, independence, and self-motivation were examples of skills and habits that students took away from the summer residential programs. The fact that lower-SES students participated in these programs and highlighted the knowledge and skills that they had acquired reflects their frame of college preparation as developing the competence, academically or behaviorally, to succeed in college.

While most lower-SES students questioned the quality of their preparation for college and thus framed college preparation as doing what they needed to do to be ready for the rigors of a college education, the few lower-SES students who attended good-quality high schools with predominantly higher-SES students were less worried about the preparation they received from their high schools. They still sought confirmation that they were prepared for college, but it was less of a concern for them. These individuals drew from the experiences of their high school alumni to assess their preparation for college. This points to the importance of the social environment of high schools in shaping how students frame college preparation. For instance, Shen, a Vietnamese American student who attended a private high school, confidently spoke about his preparation for college:

INTERVIEWER: What would you say is the most helpful thing that helps you prepare for college?

SHEN: It's just the school, everything about the school is helpful about college. That sounds very vague but I could be more specific. The teachers there are preparing you to do well in college so they make their class rigorous so that in order for you to do well in that class, you have to put in one hundred percent and they are preparing you for college because in college you have to do the same thing. I heard back from when I was talking to some of the alumni, they told me that college is easier than their high school because the education in high school is so rigorous. Because of that rigor, it prepares you to do well in college.

Shen's understanding of his own position as academically college ready is notably different than the understandings of most other lower-SES students, whose frame of college preparation left them feeling academically underprepared. Whereas most lower-SES students sought additional resources outside school to make sure they were prepared for the challenges of college, students like Shen possessed little doubt about their ability to succeed. As a result, Shen's efforts around college preparation did not involve him actively seeking opportunities to supplement what he learned in the classroom. Instead, Shen framed college preparation much like his higher-SES peers in that college preparation required that he identify opportunities to stand out among the college applicant pool.

Projecting Well-Roundedness

Other than preparing for the academic and social challenges of higher education, lower-SES students also tried to convey to colleges that they were involved with activities outside their courses. The emphasis on extracurricular activities represented another key aspect of their frame of college preparation as that of projecting themselves as well-rounded students. In contrast to their higher-SES peers, who framed engagement with extracurricular activities as a way to help them stand out from other college applicants, most lower-SES students framed these activities as opportunities to demonstrate that they were more than just high-achieving students. Lower-SES students saw involvement in extracurricular activities as a way to showcase their engagement outside school. Examples of lower-SES students' extracurricular activities include their participation in clubs and organizations and becoming involved in their communities. One student named Maria talked directly about her desire to be viewed as more than just a high-achieving student:

> MARIA: I made sure I stayed involved with my community and just doing extra things because I wanted to show them that there's more to me than being a good student. I could go above and beyond being a good student. I could do good things around my community. I could prove that I could do good things and not just be a nerd.
>
> INTERVIEWER: How did you show that again?
>
> MARIA: I did the [internship] program during the summer. I helped raise money for the school. I got involved with leadership. I got involved with organizing events with my school. Just different things. I added the internship that I had. All these things, my college application is full of a lot of extra things. I was part of ROTC [Reserve Officers' Training Corps] in freshmen year. That was interesting too but they discontinued it after that year. I have extra little things that tied into my application.

Participating in internships was one of the things that several lower-SES students pursued in their efforts to be well-rounded students. One student interned at the office of a state representative, while Maria and another student interned in science labs. Both of the science lab interns learned about the internships through their participation in college preparation programs for disadvantaged students. Maria participated in a university program intended to expose students from underrepresented populations to the medical fields. The program paired learning inside the classroom with experiences with working professionals:

I got an internship. There were twenty-four students and only five of them go to the internship. I got one which was at the Palo Alto VA [Veterans Affairs]. I was at the morgue doing autopsy. The first day the morgue supervisor was like, "Scrub in because you are going to do an autopsy." That really interested me, as weird as it sounds. That's been a lifelong goal. I got to do this at this point in life. I never thought this early. I got really good advice from that internship about the human body. It's so much different reading about it and then seeing it in real life. The organs are so fascinating. I actually got to cut the spine or vertebrae and it was good. I got to take the brain out. I got to take lectures. Actual lectures in Stanford.

The emphasis on involvement in extracurricular activities was emphasized by many lower-SES students. John, a Vietnamese American student, was one of the lower-SES students to have older siblings who had gone to a four-year college. The experiences of his older siblings reinforced the importance of involvement outside the classroom in his preparation for college. He stated, "All my siblings' involvement with school and extracurriculars made me realize that it was a really big part of it [application]." John became determined to take a rigorous course load and rack up as many extracurricular activities as possible:

I tried taking all the possible AP classes, like every one possible for every year. We are sort of at a disadvantage as well because our school is on a block schedule so that means I have to take six AP classes at the same time rather than four this semester and four next semester so it made it a lot more stressful. On top of that, I tried to put myself in the academic extracurriculars . . . mathletes, sciences, and MESA [Math, Engineering, Science, Achievement]. Also, I tried to have a healthy balance with sports as well. It basically made my school days very long, but I didn't see it that way. I saw it as a payoff for later in the future.

As part of their concerted effort to convey to colleges that they were active beyond the classroom, students also participated in community service. Community service for lower-SES students consisted primarily of providing service and assistance in their local community. Shawn, a Chinese American student, volunteered to help tutor children and adults at the local library: "I used to volunteer at the library as a tutor. A program in the West Branch to help teach about diversity. I did a lot of math and English tutoring to help people get their GED [General Education Development degree]. I also worked at a youth program. . . . As an ESL tutor, I mostly tutored almost all adults. It was very empowering but I was really scared that I'm a lot younger. I was scared that I wouldn't get the respect. It's weird. I liked it. It was fun."

The examples of Maria, John, and Shawn demonstrate how the framing of college preparation among most lower-SES students was driven by a belief in the importance of presenting themselves as well-rounded students, an approach different from that of their higher-SES peers. Lower-SES students were well aware that to get into their top choices, they needed to be more than just a high-achieving student. They sought to satisfy this understanding of college preparation by engaging in opportunities outside their courses and in the community.

Whereas most lower-SES students saw extracurricular activities as a way to establish their well-roundedness, Shen, like the higher-SES students in this study, wanted to use extracurricular activities to distinguish himself from others. In the case of Shen, everyone at his private high school was very involved. Thus he needed to separate himself from his peers by focusing on the intensity of his commitment and the positions he attained within those extracurricular activities:

> I joined a bunch of extracurricular activities. I thought that if I joined something, I should do it for four years of high school to show that I'm dedicated. I took three things and did that through high school—concert band, *LK* [literary magazine club], mock trial, and then I had tennis too. Another thing I heard about colleges is that you need to show leadership so when I was in *LK*, the literature magazine, I set a goal for myself to become the highest position so that it showed leadership in me. And I did. In my junior year, I was the co-literary editor with a senior. And now I'm the literary editor of *LK*.

Shen was among the few lower-SES students to express such a frame regarding college preparation. For most lower-SES students, their framing of college preparation was doing what they could to project competence and involvement. This led them to pursue opportunities that would equip them with skills, knowledge, grades, aptitude test scores, and extracurricular activities to demonstrate that they were well rounded.

The distinction between the approach of lower-SES students and that of the higher SES-students underscores the important role that socioeconomic status plays, not just in how much access students have to resources and opportunities but how students understand the meaning of those resources and opportunities in their lives. Even when lower-SES students like Shen possessed a frame of college preparation resembling that of his higher-SES classmates, lower-SES students are constrained in what type of activities they are able to take given their family's limited resources. Shen could only do so much given his family background, and his involvement centered primarily on activities with school clubs.

Standing Out: Projecting Passion and Autonomy

The frame of college preparation among higher-SES students was distinct from that of their lower-SES peers, highlighting the role that social class background and experiences structure the ways students understand and approach the idea of college preparation. Unlike lower-SES students who homed in on the importance of appearing well-rounded as a central strategy in their college preparation, higher-SES students framed college preparation as a matter of doing what they could to stand out from their peers. This frame was a direct result of the ultra-competitive educational environment of higher-SES schools where many students were excelling in the classroom and accumulating unprecedented extracurricular activities in preparation for college. In such a crowded academic environment, the key was to be more than just well rounded, competent, and qualified. Instead, it was to demonstrate that there was something special, unique, or exceptional about one's record of achievement and involvement.

Higher-SES students took for granted that their schools and families had equipped them with the knowledge and skills to succeed in college. They believed their learning was more than adequate to ensure a smooth transition to college. This belief in their ability to succeed at the next level was informed by the fact that high academic achievement and college preparedness were typical attributes among students at their high schools. Scott, a multiracial student, captured this view in his discussion about the academic environment of his high school: "The high school as a whole, everyone turns in their homework. Everyone comes to class every day, almost. It's like a lot of competition for grades. It's like self-motivation. People would want to get grades, not for their parents not for anything, but for themselves. The average GPA is a 3.6 or something. The point is, it's everyone. You do not admit you have a C, it's a source of shame. It's very competitive but also very supportive."

The focus among higher-SES students was less on the need to develop the skills to succeed in college and more on how they could distinguish themselves from their peers and other applicants. In their participation in activities higher-SES students sought to separate themselves from other students. Yuna, a Japanese American student, discussed the importance of this angle when describing how she saw extracurricular activities in her preparation approach:

> Doing volunteer work and striving to get better scores on the ACT. Trying to get a good score, I mean good grades in classes, take harder classes. I'm pretty sure I signed up for the leadership position in key clubs for college. I took the BCC [community college] classes for college too. Yeah, just the most stereotypical things people tell you to look good for college. I tried my best to do, which probably isn't a good motivation because you should do things you are

truly passionate about, not just to go to college. That's when I started the animal shelter because people are like, "You need to show that you weren't wasting your time and that you are doing something of good." Not that I did it for college, I also wanted to take care of cats. That's when I started thinking I need to impress whoever is going to look at my future application.

For higher-SES students, it was as much about what they did as it was about how they rationalized their activities. Many higher-SES students emphasized that what made them unique from other students was that they followed their interests and passions rather than participating in activities just to satisfy college requirements. Jaime, a white student, talked about her efforts to fulfill the general requirements of a well-rounded student while also demonstrating what was unique about her situation and activities. Jaime believed she had both common and unique attributes in her profile of extracurricular involvements: "My mom's like 'Jaime you haven't done much community service.' I don't know. I just did the things I was interested in, and at the end, when I went to see my counselor, she's like 'You have a lot of things you can talk about. Keep up your involvement and you should be fine. You have sports, leadership, involvement in community service, all throughout high school, and you have done individual things that are specific to you.'"

Higher-SES students like Jaime understood that their peers were in a similar situation—everyone was trying to accumulate as many activities as possible to prove their commitments beyond academics. If other students were just as heavily involved as they were, it would be difficult to stand out. Thus their strategy to elevate themselves from other similarly involved students was to emphasize specific activities that were unique to them. In the case of Jaime, she played softball for the high school team, she was a member of the student leadership council, and she volunteered for organizations that built homes in Oakland and Mexico. While many other students were just as busy with extracurricular commitments, Jaime emphasized that she had a unique configuration of activities that distinguished her from others. She remarked, "I like being busy. I put a lot of time into the things I am interested in. My schedule has been full during high school."

Another student, Anna, who is white, also followed this strategy. She stressed that she was different from other students because she was involved in activities that few students could put on their résumé: "I needed to be very solid academically, which for me was not a problem when I wasn't sick. And take as many AP classes as possible. In addition to that, I should do something or a lot of things outside the box. My thing ended up being Technovation and then I started a club. And then I did an internship. I feel I've done outside the box things since then. And that's kind of how I thought I would be prepared for an Ivy League."

While students like Jaime and Anna tried to be involved in as many activities as possible as a way to distinguish themselves from their peers, other students took a different route to accomplish the same objective. Rather than emphasize their configuration of activities, these other students stressed the motives behind their involvement. These students acknowledged that they did not accumulate as many as activities as others, but they believed their commitments to specific activities were just as impressive. This strategy is further elucidated in the approach of Lan, a Chinese American student, who stressed his autonomy and passion in the selection of his activities:

> I always knew that I had to get good grades. I worked hard to get all As. I didn't force myself into doing something, you know, how they say college wants you to do extracurricular activities. I didn't force myself to do anything that I didn't like. When I found Build On [a community service student organization], I really loved doing it. It also works for college so that's why I was very dedicated to the organization. I know some other people who joined ten different clubs. They forced themselves to do debate or science club. I don't think they are very happy so I didn't do that. I just wanted to pursue something that I like. And it worked out well.

Lan rationalized his involvement as reflecting his true interests and passion. He compared himself to students who were more heavily involved in activities. For Lan, it was less about the quantity of activities and more about the motivations behind the activities. By doing so, Lan highlights how higher-SES students frame their activities in ways that set them apart from others and craft a profile that is based on their individuality and uniqueness. This frame of setting oneself apart from others by stressing the quality of involvement over the quantity of involvement was also present in the preparation approach of Scott: "Do your homework. Study. Just be a good student. After that, it's a typical thing at P. High School. All your extracurricular is looked at as how they affect the college process. You want to get that before your college applications are out. You want to stick to just one sport. I obviously followed my interest but my interest, the sort of things, the popular things, also happened to be good for college. For instance, Crew [rowing sport] looks good on my college app, and it is also the sport I wanted to do."

Scott discussed his approach as participating in activities that reflected his own interests. In doing so, he distanced himself from students who were perceived as racking up activities just to fulfill college expectations. For Scott, what was important was his commitment to his specific activities. That fact that his involvements also satisfied college requirements was viewed as incidental and not necessarily intentional.

Higher-SES students sought to distinguish themselves from other college applicants as part of the approach toward college preparation. As a result of this frame of college preparation, higher-SES students focused primarily on obtaining high test scores and on their involvement in extracurricular activities, most notably academic camps, internships, and community service. Although both lower- and higher-SES students pursued these kinds of extracurricular activities, higher-SES students' participation was driven by a competitive goal. Moreover, the specific extracurricular activities that higher-SES students participated in were distinct from those of their lower-SES students, highlighting the unequal access to opportunities due to students' social class background.

In what follows, I shift from examining higher-SES framing of college preparation to look more closely at their test preparation strategies and the types of activities that they participated in as part of their strategy to stand out among their peers and other college applicants.

Academic Camps

Participating in academic camps was one of the key ways that higher-SES students pursued their goals for success within their framing of the college preparation process. About a quarter of the higher-SES students in this study participated in summer academic enrichment camps and programs during high school. These activities included camps and programs on topics that included debate, marine biology, math, science, journalism, and foreign language immersion. Most higher-SES students took part in these activities to enhance existing knowledge in these specific fields. Stephanie, a Chinese American student, was among the group of higher-SES students to spend their summers in an academic program or camp. In preparation for her role as the editor of her school newspaper, she participated in a month-long program about journalism at Northwestern University: "At my high school, my journalism teacher, she highly recommends it for people who are editor in chief. It's a five-week program. We stay on campus. There are professors from Northwestern and other lecturers and they teach us about journalism, writing articles, photography, and interviewing. It was a really fun experience."

Stephanie's opportunity to engage in an in-depth journalism program required important familial resources that were more likely to be available to higher-income families. Her desire to pursue this type of program reflects the importance that higher-SES students attached to these types of activities as part of their understanding of college preparation, specifically how to make them stand out.

Another example of this can be seen in the academic camps that Amy pursued. While most students engaged in a different summer academic activity each year, Amy, a Chinese American student, was among the few who participated in the same activity for multiple summers. Her passion for math led her to math camps for consecutive summers. What Amy remembered most about her participation in math camps was the people she met and how they helped to normalize her enthusiasm for a specific subject area:

> Math camp, it's a five-week residence program. They change location every year. First year it was in Lewis and Clark College in Portland. Second year was in Puget Sound University in Washington. They are very much based on the idea of being independent and free to choose when and what to learn. There are four classes offered every single day, and classes go through weeklong blocks. And every week, you get to choose a class for each block or you can choose not to go to class. People go there to learn of course. I think it was very much like the college experience. I haven't been to college so I'm not sure. You are there because you want to learn. It's nice to be surrounded by people who are passionate about a subject. I liked math before but I didn't know what liking math meant until I went there. They are wonderful people. It's a very carefree environment, people are very supportive. It's an international program. All sorts of different people. You can be as crazy or not crazy as you like.

Whereas lower-SES students participated in academic programs to prepare them for doing well in their classes or in preparation for the rigors of college courses, higher-SES students like Amy perceived their involvement in similar activities as more of a social experience than an academic experience. Higher-SES students did not question their preparedness for college. As a result they remembered academic activities less in terms of the skills they gained and more for the social experiences they accumulated.

As the cases of Amy and Stephanie illustrate, some of these academic camps and programs took place out of state. Without the economic resources of their parents, these experiences would not have been possible. Even the experiences that are local or in state still required significant fees so these are activities that would not be accessible to students lacking financial means. Though higher-SES students may not explicitly link these activities to their frame of college preparation, given their desire to stand out, it is clear that these remarkable activities certainly fit in with their college preparation approach.

Internships

Internships represented another common method that higher-SES students sought to gain a competitive edge, and almost half of the higher-SES students participated in some type of internships while in high school. These internships were situated in nonprofit organizations, government agencies, universities, and companies. They were often quite prestigious and were frequently obtained through family networks. Stephanie, for example, was able to secure an internship at a software company founded by her father: "The summers before ninth and tenth grade, I worked at this computer software company. The company, they make websites for realtors. You know how you can send mass emails to people, I would sign up with a mass email account and I would manage those accounts for that summer. From tenth to eleventh grade, I worked there too. That year, they were designing software to build your own websites so I was helping out with that."

Learning about or securing internships through parents was a common occurrence. In fact, this was the typical way that most higher-SES students accessed such opportunities. Nick, a white student, described how his mother, who worked for a health care company, passed on to him opportunities about internships:

NICK: This past summer, I worked at a research institute in a biomedical research lab at Oakland Children's Hospital.

INTERVIEWER: How did you hear about it?

NICK: My mom works at the research institute. I was thinking last summer that I want to do something that gears me for college like an internship. My mom emails me about this opportunity that the research institute does. I decided to apply. I'm interested in science and medicine. I'm not sure if I want to be a doctor so I want to explore opportunities in the lab.

INTERVIEWER: What were you doing?

NICK: There's a lot of responsibilities. I had to fill forms to start working. A lot of preparation. A lot of the research they do, you have to be responsible and know how to not contaminate, a lot of biohazards. Research might be confidential, a lot of security. I wasn't working on any top secret. You can't just walk into a lab and press any button. I was given more independence toward the end of the summer in the lab. I was doing some of the brunt work. I was contributing to this multiyear project.

Another student who secured an internship via their parents was James, a Chinese American student, who worked in the lab of a Nobel laureate faculty at the local university one summer, an opportunity that he was able to secure because of his mother's connection to the professor. He recalled that it took a while for the opportunity to materialize: "Yes, I emailed the guy. My mom was a postdoc with him way back then. I emailed him and it took a year to make it happen."

While parents often served as the connections to opportunities, some higher-SES students did not have that privilege. Instead, they took it upon themselves to identify and apply to internships. Some internships were public in that they were advertised. For other internships, students created the internships themselves by inquiring about opportunities. This latter situation was that of Mary, a Chinese American student, who emailed professors looking for opportunities to work with them during the summers: "I wanted to do botany at that time. I actually emailed the professor. I'm like 'Hey, I'm a sophomore, these are my grades, I really want to work in your lab, would you take me?' And he's like, 'Yes.'"

Whether it was through their own doing or through the social connections of their parents, or both, higher-SES students were able to access unique opportunities to explore their career interests. The knowledge about such opportunities, the confidence to even inquire about internships, and the social connections to get their foot in the door are a testament to how growing up in a higher-SES environment gave middle- and upper-middle-class children access to valuable experiences to further their academic and career pursuits. These exceptional opportunities certainly enable higher-SES students to distinguish themselves from other high-achieving students.

Community Service

A third important activity that higher-SES students pursued in ways that advanced their framing of college preparation was to engage in volunteer activities. These activities ranged from assisting organizations in their hometown to going abroad to provide services. Jessica, a white student, was part of a program that provided tutoring to young children locally:

> I'm involved with a program called Venture Crew, it's run through the Boy Scouts of America. It allows high school students to take charge of community service opportunity. It's a lot of youth leadership. There are many projects and you choose. I do a lot of tutoring with refugees from Burma. A lot of them are in third or fourth grade or even high school. There's a woman, she opens her house, she's one of the doctors at a local clinic, and she opens her house to them. On Tuesday night she has all these children, and we help them with their work.

Community service in which students volunteered with organizations or activities in their local vicinity was common. For instance, Emily, a Chinese American student, volunteered at her local senior community center once a month, while Denise, a white student, committed her time to the city zoo and a local animal shelter. Performing community service abroad during the summer was also something that was typical. These experiences abroad were expensive, and students either fundraised for it or had their parents foot the bill. Jaime contributed to building homes in her hometown and traveled to Mexico with her church to build homes: "I'm also involved with community service. This Mexico mission trip is through the community church. Basically everyone at church does it no matter what religion they are. It's been really fun. I've also been involved with our Venture Crew, a club at our school; we go and build things. We go through a program called Rebuilding Together Oakland, and we go to the local area and help rebuild houses for low-income people or people with disabilities, and it's been very fun."

Some of the community service projects performed by higher-SES students were similar to those undertaken by their lower-SES peers in that they only required time and effort. Others, such as those in which students went abroad or had to acquire materials, required that students have the financial means to participate. While some higher-SES students fundraised, this sometimes was not enough. Consequently, some students relied on their parents to finance their community service participation. This once again highlights the role that familial resources plays in helping students secure valuable experiences that enable students to stand apart from their peers.

Test Preparation

A fourth kind of activity that higher-SES students engaged in that also reflects the framing of college preparation were activities related to test preparation. Whereas lower-SES students viewed their test scores as a reflection of their competence to succeed in college, higher-SES students viewed it as a way to get ahead of their peers. As part of their frame of college preparation, higher-SES students sought to get as close to perfection as possible on their test performance. About half of all higher-SES students received private instruction on the SATs, ACTs, or AP exams, while the rest of the higher-SES students prepared by themselves. Of those who relied on private instruction, most received one-on-one instruction with a private tutor. Macy, a white student, was one of these students, and she had multiple tutors:

MACY: For my SAT tutor, I had a chemistry tutor last year. I had calculus and physics tutors this year, an hour a week.
INTERVIEWER: How helpful are those tutors?
MACY: Super helpful. I raised my SAT 300 points. They guaranteed a 300 points increase for your score compared to your PSAT. I was sick the day I took my PSAT so I'm not very sure how accurate it was. It was pretty bad when I was taking it. I got like the mid-1900s, it's not a bad score, it's not the best score. It's testing strategies and techniques.

James, who is Chinese American, utilized group instruction lessons from a private company as well as private individual tutors:

When I took the ACT the first time, I got a 27 and I was like I should get some tutoring. Go to Princeton Review. They bumped it up to 29. It was not good enough. I went to a private tutor. These are very expensive things that my mom was willing to pay for. All you have to do is take three tests per week for ten weeks and that's what I did. My sophomore year, actually, on the plane ride there and sometimes in the hotel, I would do three per week for ten weeks. I would end my last practice before the actual test. My score rose from a 29 to a 35. I've gotten a few 36 on some practice tests. It was pretty difficult. I would wake up at four o'clock in the morning, it's a 3.5-hour practice test.

James relied on private instructions, but it was ultimately his commitment to a grueling study plan that landed him the score that he aimed for. For Emily, a Chinese American student, her parents placed her in a summer camp program designed specifically for SAT preparation:

> EMILY: During junior year, I had SAT camp. I just stayed home and studied. My dad makes me study for classes. I end up just slacking off. Physics prep classes and math prep class during the summer.
>
> INTERVIEWER: SAT camp? What did it consist of?
>
> EMILY: It consisted of prepping in every subject, and quizzes every week, three days a week, for the last five weeks, it was only on Saturdays. It was pretty intense.

Higher-SES students who did not receive private lessons prepared by reading test strategy books and taking multiple practice exams. Most of these students believed that their courses had prepared them well, and they just needed to supplement them with individual practice. Louise, a Chinese American student, was one such student. Her approach consisted of taking multiple practice exams until she was satisfied with her results and comfortable in her ability to do well on the actual exam.

> LOUISE: I had to study a lot on my own, especially on the SAT. I would find time for myself and open the bluebook and do practice tests. I did maybe ten of them. Through that I just prepared for it. That was tough. When it came to test, I had to be a lot more disciplined and on task.
>
> INTERVIEWER: How long did you study for the test?
>
> LOUISE: I studied a lot. For the SAT, I started studying in my sophomore year and then as it got closer, I would increase my hours in the day and increase my tests but I was always doing vocabulary flashcards and math problems.

The test preparation approaches of some higher-SES students here resembled those of their lower-SES peers. There were students from both groups that supplemented their test preparation instruction with their own studying. What was different was that higher-SES students seemed to have a more systematic way of conducting their self-preparation. Moreover, whereas the source and quality of the test preparation instruction varied from one lower-SES student to another, higher-SES students consistently received instruction from individuals or organizations specialized in test preparation. Higher-SES students were more likely to have access to individual one-on-one test preparation instruction.

Conclusion

In analyzing the preparation approaches and activities of students, it is clear that higher-SES students felt very secure in their ability to do well in college. They were confident that their high schools and families adequately prepared them for the transition to college. They rarely spoke at all about needing to do things to make sure they were ready for the rigors of college. For higher-SES students, college preparation was less about preparation for success in college; rather, it represented their efforts to enhance their admission profiles. They framed college preparation as doing what they could to stand out among other students as they competed for admission spots. In their discussion about their approach, many higher-SES students sought to distance themselves from the preparations of other students by emphasizing how they engaged in activities that reflected their unique interests and passions. In doing so, they were projecting their distinctiveness from other students and emphasizing their autonomy in their selection of activities.

The approach and activities of lower-SES students, on the other hand, were geared toward meeting the expectations of the typical qualified college applicant. They framed college preparation as acquiring the necessary skill sets to succeed in college and demonstrating their engagement in activities beyond the classroom. Many lower-SES students expressed worries about the quality of their preparation in high school for success in college. Consequently, lower-SES students searched for ways to develop the skills to succeed in college and to project to colleges that they were competent and well-rounded. Students became involved in activities like academic programs to receive the academic assistance to do well in key subject matters and to learn more about college admissions and the necessary college skill sets. Outside academic preparation, lower-SES students became involved in extracurricular activities with the understanding that they needed to demonstrate that they were well-rounded students.

Social class differences were not just apparent in the preparation approaches of students but also in the types of activities that they actually participated in. Whereas higher-SES students frequently took part in academic camps, lower-SES students were typically involved in academic preparation programs. Academic camps consisted of activities geared toward helping students enhance their skills or abilities in a specific subject area. Academic programs, on the other hand, such as the college preparation programs for lower-SES students, referred to activities that supported students more holistically from their coursework to preparation for college. Whereas academic camps were typically fee based, academic programs were available at no cost to students from disadvantaged backgrounds. When it came to test preparation activities, higher-SES students typically utilized private fee-based instruction that consisted of personalized one-on-one instruction. For lower-SES students, test preparation instruction was usually offered free of charge through their academic programs and sometimes their high schools via a group instruction format.

Outside academic activities and test preparation activities, higher-SES students were more likely to become involved in community service activities, internships, and musical groups. Higher-SES students participated in community service activities, some of which took place in communities abroad; they participated in musical groups on and off campus, performing across the region and even across the country. Many higher-SES students became involved in internships over the summer.

Social class differences in preparation approaches and involvement in activities can lead to inequity in the admission process if admissions officers are not aware of how inequality in resources contributes to distinct profiles for lower-SES and higher-SES students. Highly ranked colleges typically look for students who are deeply involved in extracurricular activities and who demonstrate initiative and passion for what they do. Higher-SES students were aware of such criteria, and they had the resources to meet those requirements. They also possessed the language to discuss their activities to fit in with what colleges desired from their student body. Lower-SES students, on the other hand, focused more on how they fit in, how they were competent and qualified. In the typical situation in which there are more qualified applicants than there are available admission spots, unless colleges and universities take into account the social and economic backgrounds of applicants, higher-SES students will ultimately end up being admitted far more often than lower-SES students due to the fit between what these colleges seek and what higher-SES students are able to project. If top colleges continue to prioritize admitting students with distinguished records of accomplishments and activities without taking into account the resources students have at their disposal to attain those records, top colleges will inevitably privilege the experiences of higher-SES students at the expense of lower-SES students.

This is because extracurricular involvement is heavily biased toward those with financial and social capital; in other words, higher-SES students. In her widely cited study on social class differences in childhood upbringing, Annette Lareau (2002) shows how middle- and upper-middle-class families place their children in multiple organized activities that range from sports to music and academic programs. Children from low-income and working-class families do not have as many opportunities to participate in organized activities. As top colleges consider whom to admit, it is important that they recognize the different frames of college preparation that students utilize and avoid penalizing qualified students who lack access to financial and social capital that can enhance their body of extracurricular activities.

3

Schemas of Colleges

• •

Martina is a Mexican American student from a family of a comparatively lower socioeconomic status. She recently graduated from a high school in which 90 percent of the students participated in the free or reduced-price lunch program, which is a good indicator of the concentration of students who, like Martina, came from low-income backgrounds. During her time as a student there, the high school underwent a great deal of turmoil, including frequent administrative turnovers and the hiring of inexperienced teachers. Not surprisingly, Martina's high school provided her with only limited exposure to colleges. When the school did present information about colleges, it was primarily about eligibility requirements and less about the consequences of attending one type of college over others. She recalled the colleges that sent representatives to her high school campus to recruit students: "A couple of UCs [Universities of California] and a lot of schools that I really didn't know like Alameda Art school. It was a lot of art schools. And then a lot of schools that aren't well-known."

Had Martina depended only on her high school for information about college, she would have made her decision about what to do after high school with the idea that four-year colleges, two-year colleges, and vocational schools were all appropriate options for her. However, Martina was also involved with multiple programs that assisted students with college preparation and exploration, and these programs influenced how she viewed her options. One of these programs was UB, a federally funded program whose mission is to prepare first-generation and underrepresented students for college. Martina described how the program emphasized four-year colleges in California, ranging from public UCs and CSUs [California State Universities] to some in-state private colleges. This exposure in the program shifted Martina's thinking about college. She stopped thinking that two-year colleges and vocational schools would be appropriate for her. Instead, she became increasingly focused on four-year colleges.

While the program classified California's four-year colleges as appropriate options, Martina engaged in her own process of evaluation to decide which options were the right ones for her. One of the important factors she utilized for deciding where she would apply to college was whether or not she had visited the college: "I only wanted to apply to the ones that I have been to," she said. "I feel like it didn't serve any purpose for me to apply to schools that I've never been to because if I got accepted, I really wouldn't go there because I don't know what the school was like. So I only applied to schools that I have visited before."

Martina narrowed down the list of appropriate four-year colleges to those that reflected her preferences and that she was familiar with. For Martina, college visits gave her a sense of comfort about the type of environment she would be getting herself into. In the absence of a visit, just reading about a college was not a sufficient reason to apply to that college. She ended up applying to four UCs, four CSUs, and three private universities, including Stanford, all in California.

Stephanie, a higher-SES Chinese American student, attended a competitive academic high school. Less than 1 percent of students at her high school are low-income. Her family moved into the local community just so that she could take advantage of the highly rated educational system. When asked to discuss the types of higher education institutions that students at her high school usually attended, Stephanie described colleges that spanned across the United States: "There are a lot of people who go to UCs and some CSUs because in-state tuition is cheaper. A lot of people go to small liberal arts throughout the country. Some aim for the Ivies. . . . Maybe because it's a small high school that people feel more comfortable in a small liberal arts college. There's a lot of random ones like Bowdoin, Davidson, Macalester, Bates, Wellesley. There's a ton. There are so many people who went to these small colleges."

Stephanie was thus exposed to a selection of predominantly top colleges across the United States in the form of UCs, private research universities, and small liberal arts colleges. While she perceived all these colleges as appropriate for her, she narrowed down the list to those that suited her needs and desires. She emphasized large schools because she sought a change from the small school feel of her high school. She relied heavily on multiple college ranking lists, identifying those universities known for their top engineering programs. Based on these considerations, she ultimately applied to the UCs, in-state private universities, Ivy League universities, and out-of-state liberal arts colleges.

Martina and Stephanie's different approaches to considering and selecting colleges reflect a larger pattern of divergence among lower-SES students and higher-SES students. These divergences are influenced by a number of factors, most notably high schools and college preparation programs. This chapter examines the organizational cultures of high schools and college preparation programs in terms of how they convey possible choices to their students. Thinking organizationally about the influence of schools and programs draws our attention to the ways in which decision making is structured by shared understanding and rules within these settings (Dimaggio and Powell 1991). These organizations—in this case high schools and college preparation programs— shape students' decision making and actions through the imposition of cognitive and interpretive schemas—ways of making sense of the social world through a system of classification or categorization of people and objects (Lamont, Beljean, and Clair 2014).

As the experiences of students discussed in this chapter highlight, high schools and college preparation programs present students with different configurations of colleges—which represent schemas—that students then use to identify and sort out colleges and universities, resulting in the creation of boundaries among the different options. Depending on the schema, students would recognize some options but ignore others. Among the recognized options, there is typically a hierarchy of preferred choices at the top and undesirable options at the bottom. These kinds of schemas facilitate and constrain students' decision making—the configuration of colleges make the college application process manageable, but they close off certain options.

Through their high schools, higher-SES students were presented with a *selective colleges anywhere* schema whereby selective colleges, especially private ones, from across the country (e.g., top UCs, selective private liberal arts colleges, and Ivy League universities) were promoted, whereas low-ranked and nonselective colleges (e.g., CSUs, two-year colleges, and low-ranked UCs) were stigmatized. In contrast to higher-SES students, most lower-SES students were exposed to a selection of colleges that reflected a *local postsecondary education* schema or an *in-state four-year college* schema via their high schools and college preparation programs. In the *local postsecondary education* schema, students were encouraged to pursue additional schooling at nearby higher education institutions, whether it was vocational/trade schools, two-year colleges, or four-year colleges. In the *in-state four-year college* schema, any type of four-year colleges in the state (e.g., UCs and CSUs), regardless of selectivity, was emphasized, whereas two-year and vocational schools were discouraged. In both configurations, out-of-state colleges were rarely discussed and essentially ignored.

While these schemas in the form of configurations of colleges structured how students thought about higher education, students did not unthinkingly accept these schemas of college. Instead, students also engaged in their own process of classification and categorization by drawing on their understandings, knowledge, and experiences to determine which ones among the appropriate colleges were the right fit for them. The key difference between appropriate and right colleges is that appropriate colleges denote a range of acceptable colleges for a group of students from a specific organization, while the right colleges represent a subset of those appropriate colleges that is reflective of the preferences of each individual. Both the schemas and the criteria students utilized to select specific colleges to submit college applications were heavily influenced by the social class–based environments of their schools, college preparation programs, and their experiences outside these organizations.

Lower-SES Students

Most lower-SES students, in keeping with the schemas that their high schools and college preparation programs presented to them, did not submit an application to any colleges outside California. These students fall into one of two groups: One group consists of students who were primarily informed about in-state colleges through their schools and college preparation programs. It did not occur to these students to seriously consider out-of-state colleges because they knew very little about such colleges. In other words, the schemas of colleges to which they were exposed ignored out-of-state colleges, sending a message to students that such options were not appropriate for them. The second group of students received information and were encouraged to submit applications to colleges beyond California, but their apprehensions about living in unfamiliar environments far from home and family ties forced them to ultimately abandon these colleges.

In contrast, the several lower-SES students who did submit applications to out-of-state colleges were typically those who had attended high school with other higher-SES students, or they had been in environments outside California. These experiences enabled them to view out-of-state colleges as more desirable than did their lower-SES peers. Most responded by applying to out-of-state colleges.

In comparison to their Black and Hispanic peers, Asian American students from lower-SES backgrounds were more likely to attend schools that put more resources into and emphasis on exposing students to four-year colleges. Moreover, though almost all lower-SES students who were interviewed for this book participated in college preparation programs, Asian American students were more likely to participate in the selective programs that sought to place low-income students in the nation's top private colleges and universities. As a consequence, lower-SES Asian American students were more likely to be exposed to a *selective college anywhere* schema. Their Black and Hispanic counterparts, on the other hand, were more likely to encounter the *in-state four-year college* schema and the *any local postsecondary education* schema that emphasized colleges and opportunities locally or within the state. Nevertheless, although these different trends among racial/ethnic groups point to the role of other social factors in the college selection processes, they do not change the overall—and diverging—patterns of college selection between lower- and higher-SES students.

Application to In-State Colleges Only: Schemas That Ignore Out-of-State Colleges

John, a Chinese American student, attended a high school in which 80 percent of students were in the free and reduced-price lunch program. John was well aware of the perception that others have of students at his high school: "Commonly at my high school, there's that stereotype that a lot of kids will go to community college." Many students at his high school struggled with completing their college applications. Fortunately, John did not encounter such issues as he actively sought out school resources. He asked his teachers about their experiences in college. Through this, he learned about two of the top universities in California: Stanford and UC Berkeley. The school's career center proved to be the most helpful in exposing him to colleges: "The career center, every two weeks, they had a guest college come in. I remembered they had [UC] Berkeley, UCLA, [UC] San Diego, back to back. And then they'll always get a representative to come and talk to the students to have the students get a better understanding of the applications and stuff like that. It really was informative to get to know the UCs better because it was the most overwhelming [application] so to have someone come and talk to us it made it seem less scary to apply."

In addition to the UCs, the career center also brought in representatives from the state universities (CSUs). Only a few private colleges made it to his school. By bringing these colleges to campus, the high school deemed them as appropriate options for their students. John drew from this *in-state four-year college* schema to make his decision about where he should apply to college. To narrow down the list of appropriate options, he drew on a set of criteria that emphasized financial cost, distance from home, and academic programs in engineering. In regard to distance, John preferred "local schools [with] UCLA being the furthest." Out-of-state colleges were not part of the schema he received from his school, but he was aware of Ivy League universities. John decided against applying to the Ivy Leagues because he thought media portrayals "make it seem like to get into Harvard it's hard. It's going to cost a huge amount and even though you are low-income, you could be affected by it." In the end, John applied to four UCs, four CSUs, and a couple of in-state private universities, including Stanford.

Sofia, who is Mexican American, was another student who was exposed to a schema that recognized only in-state colleges. Sofia attended a college preparatory high school for students from disadvantaged backgrounds in which two-thirds of the students participated in the reduced-price lunch program. At the school, Sofia was exposed to an *in-state four-year college* schema. All graduating students were required to submit at least a college application to a four-year college. Despite the focus on four-year colleges, the school primarily emphasized CSUs. Her participation in UB, the college preparation program, exposed her to more colleges beyond the CSU. This program enabled her to learn about and visit several UCs: "We got introduced to UC Berkeley so we are very familiar with Berkeley. But in SoCal [Southern California], they took us to different UCs, privates, and state schools so we got a chance to see the different campuses."

Despite not being introduced to out-of-state colleges by way of her school or the college preparation program, Sofia and other lower-SES students were not ignorant about top out-of-state private colleges. They knew about these prestigious universities, and some entertained thoughts of applying to them. However, when these colleges are not part of the schema that students are exposed to, such colleges do not receive the attention they deserve, and students come to view these colleges as not for them. Here, Sofia recounted her thought process about an out-of-state college: "I was going to apply to Penn [University of Pennsylvania], but I looked at the area and it's way too far and I don't really see myself that far. I like California. . . . I don't want to get out of my community or California. I don't want to go far away. I don't mind going a little far away. But I really don't want to go out of state. I just see myself here where I grew up."

Sofia ultimately applied to four UCs, four CSUs, and a couple of private universities. In addition to distance from home, among the criteria that she considered was the availability of financial aid, the majors, and whether she will fit in as a student of color. She dismissed a private university in California because she was worried about her sense of belonging there: "I also saw the people who go there and it's not as diverse. And I don't really want to be surrounded by people who are very competitive, and it doesn't have people of color because I grew up with people of color." For Sofia, the prestige of the college mattered less than the majors available: "It doesn't matter what school you get into as long as you get your major, you are going to learn." These considerations influenced her college application decisions.

John and Sofia represent students whose high schools and college preparation programs did not recognize out-of-state colleges as appropriate options for them. While they came across out-of-state colleges beyond these organizational settings, the limited understanding they had about such colleges constrained their applications to in-state colleges. The difference between learning about out-of-state colleges by oneself and encountering them via schemas is that schemas represent external validation that students are capable of gaining admission to and succeeding in these higher education institutions. From organizational staff working to expose students to these colleges to the presence of postsecondary recruiters on campus to alumni who have matriculated to these colleges, schemas represent more than just information about colleges. Schemas reflect a process of inculcating in students appropriate college options.

Application to In-State Colleges Only: The Absence of Experiences beyond California

By presenting out-of-state colleges as potential options to their students, high schools and academic programs can increase the chances that a student will apply to one of those colleges. However, as the experiences of another group of lower-SES students demonstrate, just because organizations like high schools and academic programs include out-of-state colleges in their schemas, it does not mean that lower-SES students will necessarily submit applications to these colleges. Even when academic programs and high schools deemed out-of-state college as suitable for them, some lower-SES students did not find these colleges desirable due to financial concerns and perceived fears that resulted from the lack of experiences in out-of-state environments. Students were not comfortable with the prospect of living in an environment that they considered too different from where they grew up.

Andrea, a Chinese American student, represents one of those students. She attended a school that had over 75 percent of its students enrolled in the free lunch program. However, the school was considered a middle-tier public high school, and it drew students from different parts of the city. Through teachers and campus assemblies, the school instilled in their students a college-going mindset. The school brought in individuals to speak about specific colleges during assemblies, impressed upon students the UC requirements so that students "knew them by heart," and held college fairs, which had representatives from the UCs, CSUs, local private colleges, and historically Black colleges and universities (HBCUs). The school also took students on college visits to nearby UCs.

Andrea was also part of CT, a college preparation program aimed at getting more high-achieving, low-income students into some of the nation's most selective colleges. Given its mission, the program worked to help students recognize college possibilities beyond those that exist in California. In the program, Andrea was exposed to a *selective college anywhere* schema. She learned about a host of out-of-state private colleges, many of which are liberal arts colleges. Public and private research universities in California, such as the UCs, Stanford, and USC, were encouraged along with small liberal arts colleges, such as Occidental College. Outside of California, the focus was on small liberal arts colleges across the South, Midwest, and East Coast.

Though she was exposed to out-of-state liberal arts colleges, Andrea was not interested in them. While the program helped her to recognize such colleges as appropriate options, she evaluated the desirability of those college choices by bringing in her own experiences and understandings:

ANDREA: I always knew that I wouldn't want to be in Oakland, but I probably wouldn't want to be out of California.

INTERVIEWER: Is there a reason for why you don't consider out-of-state colleges?

ANDREA: I guess weather wise. It's really cold out there.

INTERVIEWER: You've been out there before?

ANDREA: I watch a lot of travel shows. Actually I've never been to the East Coast, which is weird. The idea of New York kind of scares me. It feels like really large, rich buildings and dark alleys.

INTERVIEWER: Other things besides the weather that make you throw out going out of state?

ANDREA: I think also culturewise. California, there are so many of us. We are really diverse.

INTERVIEWER: What do you worry about going outside California?

ANDREA: I guess attitudewise. People in California are pretty open minded. I like that sort of environment so I'd rather be in that environment for a little until I want to go out and look at things.

Andrea engaged in her own process of evaluation to determine which colleges were the right fit for her. She saw a major departure in terms of the social and physical environment between California colleges and out-of-state colleges. California represented proximity to racial and ethnic diversity, attributes that she preferred. In doing so, Andrea drew on an evaluative frame that separated California colleges from out-of-state colleges based on environmental and social desirability. Her lack of experience beyond California made her rely on the media to form unfavorable opinions about the prospect of attending an out-of-state college. She submitted applications to the UCs, CSUs, and a couple of private in-state universities.

Shawn, a Chinese American student, attended a socioeconomically mixed high school. At his school, there were college counselors who helped students identify and apply to college. While the ratio of students to college counselors was so large that it was difficult to meet with them, Shawn was once called into a counselor's office to talk about colleges that might fit him. He recalled, "One of them pulled me in with my friends. 'What's your SAT, GPA? You are an okay fit.'" At the school, students like him were exposed to a *selective college anywhere* schema; they were encouraged to attend a four-year college, but there was a hierarchy of preferred colleges. Here he discussed the colleges that are considered inferior for students from his high school: "I think the stigma of being a CSU is one of the reasons. . . . Okay . . . it's because the rankings system is CC, CSU, UC. It's more known that UC are higher ranked than CSU. They are harder to get into. . . . At the CSU, the GPA is lower and SAT is a lot lower. That's one of the reasons why people don't want to go there."

While lower-ranked colleges like the CSUs and two-year colleges were considered off limits, top colleges across the United States and even outside the United States were proper options. This was evident in how he talked about where students applied to college: "Some people are applying to all the UCs as safeties and the privates like Duke, Claremont McKenna, Rice, just a lot of the Claremont colleges like Harvey Mudd. Those and some that applied to very prestigious universities. I have some friends that are applying overseas as well. I have one that is applying to a French university, NYU [New York University], someone is going to UBC [University of British Columbia]. It's all over the place."

Yet, when it came to his decision, Shawn only applied to all the UCs. He avoided the CSU system because of the stigma attached to it given that he was a high-achieving student. But he did not follow the paths of some of his peers in submitting applications to out-of-state colleges. As a lower-SES student, he was concerned about the cost of pursuing college outside California: "I didn't want to go out of state. I don't want to pay out of state tuition." Regarding the life outside California, he stated, "I lived in California all my life. People on the East Coast, I heard are very rushed. People are really relaxed here."

Both Shawn and Andrea had SAT scores and GPAs that would have put them in competition for admission into prestigious universities around the United States. However, despite being exposed to those top universities in the *selective college anywhere* schema that they encountered in their high schools and programs, both Shawn and Andrea opted for in-state universities due to specific constraints connected to their family's socioeconomic circumstances and their own experiences. Shawn and Andrea's decision making reflects broader patterns among other lower-SES students and shows how exposure to and knowledge of colleges is not sufficient for many students to apply to top universities beyond California. For these students, constraints beyond information must also be addressed. Some of these other factors, in addition to information, that can more effectively encourage lower-SES students to submit applications to colleges beyond a specific geographic area like California are addressed in the next two sections.

Application to Both In- and Out-Of-State Colleges: The Role of Out-of-State Experiences

The few lower-SES students who did apply to out-of-state colleges were ones who had experiences in out-of-state environments or who had attended schools that consisted predominantly of higher-SES students. The experiences and understandings these lower-SES students brought to their decision making gave rise to an evaluative frame that depicted out-of-state colleges as appropriate and also desirable. One such student is Madison, a Laotian American student, who attended a school in which 85 percent of the students qualified for free or reduced-price lunch. Given the challenges that her school faced in getting students to graduate from high school, she rarely brought up the support of her school in the college exploration process.

Madison's decision to apply to out-of-state colleges stemmed from her participation in many programs that not only exposed her to a *selective college anywhere* schema but also gave her opportunities to experience activities and colleges outside California. One such program took her backpacking in Seattle and then in Virginia. According to Madison, the program "helps low-income students gain experiences that are usually out of reach." Another program took her abroad to Nicaragua and Peru to learn about social and environmental issues affecting people in those countries. These experiences away from home allowed her to embrace being in situations or places different from her own: "It's important for people from Asian backgrounds to go and see what's out there. My parents were overprotective; they have such limited ideas. Growing up in that environment, you are limited to different ideas and you don't know what's out there. I thought it was important that I stepped out and discovered things on my own."

Madison's involvement in the college preparation program CT spurred her interest in small private colleges outside California. CT offered students a *selective college anywhere* schema, enabling Madison to recognize colleges outside California as appropriate options for her. However, had it not been for her out-of-state experiences, she would not have seriously considered such colleges. The experiences and understandings that resulted from her trips outside California allowed her to evaluate these colleges within a context that made them desirable. In addition to being introduced to private colleges outside California, she was able to participate in several trips to out-of-state colleges. These visits solidified her interest to attend a small college:

> My junior year, I visited with CT, UPenn [University of Pennsylvania] and Swarthmore. That was another time I realized I wanted a small school, but on the East Coast. I put all that together. I compared being at UPenn versus Swarthmore. The environment at Swarthmore felt more intimate and closer to me. UPenn is not exactly small, it's big for a private college. And then there's a fly-in program so I visited Bryn Mawr in Pennsylvania, an all-women's college. I really thought I wanted to go to an all-women's college so I almost committed to them on the spot. I think it's important for students to know what's out there, to actually visit those colleges. It's so different to read about it versus visiting them.

These college visits cultivated her interest in pursuing higher education outside California. The intimacy of small colleges motivated her to prioritize these colleges in her college application. She initially perceived small colleges as similar to a high school, where she would run into the same people every day. However, the visits helped dispel this notion, and she learned about the benefits that could accrue from attending such a college. Madison ended up applying to almost thirty colleges, consisting of in-state colleges (UCs, CSUs, private colleges) and multiple out-of-state private colleges, particularly liberal arts colleges.

Anthony, an African American student, was another lower-SES student who also applied to out-of-state colleges. Over 80 percent of students at his high school qualified for the free lunch program. The school also had a negative reputation, something that Anthony was well aware of, but which he felt was not warranted: "There's violence around the school but not inside it. It has a reputation of being violent. There's fights and violence but it doesn't get into the school. People think it's a bad school but that's not true. . . . Now we have legitimate AP [advanced placement] teachers, it has improved since I've been here."

Through his attending college fairs at the school and around his city, Anthony was exposed to a *selective college anywhere* schema of colleges that not only included in-state four-year colleges but also out-of-state colleges like private research universities and HBCUs. While he recognized such colleges as appropriate options for him, it was his participation in the UB program that allowed him to evaluate out-of-state colleges more positively. Via the UB program, he was able to go to Hawaii for one summer and participate in a sister program there. This trip sparked his interest in exploring different places, an experience that was key to his decision to apply to out-of-state colleges:

INTERVIEWER: Tell me about those experiences.

ANTHONY: Hawaii was funny. It was really slow compared to everything else. They even say I talk too fast. This is normal for California people. They say, "You talk too fast, walk too fast, think too fast." They said I talked weird, food I eat is weird. It was a culture shock but it was fun. I enjoyed the life, it was peaceful. It was fun learning about different places.

INTERVIEWER: Some students experience this, and it makes them hesitant to go back. For you it's different?

ANTHONY: It's fun. I don't know. It's so different from what I'm used to. I don't like the same thing over and over again. That's really boring to me.

Anthony's summer in Hawaii allowed him to experience a different way of life. The pace of life and the people he interacted with in Hawaii interrupted what he had been familiar with. In doing so, the culture shock he experienced also disrupted the monotony of life. He came to embrace the changes that came along with being in a new environment. This understanding of what it meant to live away from home in a new environment made applying to colleges beyond California more desirable. He applied to a prominent private research university in New York and several HBCUs in addition to the UCs and CSUs.

Experiences in out-of-state environments played an important role in Anthony's and Madison's decisions to apply to out-of-state colleges. While they both initially experienced culture shock in these environments, they eventually learned to accept and embrace living in a new environment and engaging with people who come from different backgrounds. They recognized that by putting themselves in new situations, they were also opening themselves up to further opportunities for growth and maturity. This newfound perspective provided them with the confidence to think about living outside California, a necessary element in their decision to apply to out-of-state colleges. Thus, out-of-state college schemas, when combined with positive experiences in out-of-state environments, helped lower-SES students to view appropriate colleges as the right colleges for them as well.

Application to Both In- and Out-of-State Colleges: The Role of High-Quality Schools

While most lower-SES students attended schools that consisted primarily of other lower-SES students, three of the lower-SES students in this research attended schools that largely enrolled higher-SES students. Two students attended what is considered the top public school in their city, and one student attended a private school. All three students were Asian American. These lower-SES students made sense of higher education via a *selective college anywhere* schema that classified both in- and out-of-state competitive four-year colleges as appropriate for them. Of the three students who attended these high-quality schools, two applied to out-of-state colleges. While these students did not have out-of-state experiences, they attended schools in which application to out-of-state colleges was common. The two students who applied to out-of-state colleges were able to draw on their experience at schools with significant concentrations of higher-SES students to evaluate out-of-state colleges positively.

Shen, a Vietnamese American student, attended a private high school via a scholarship for low-income students. At the high school, where tuition was more than $20,000 a year, students were expected to matriculate to a four-year college. Students met in groups and individually with the school college counselors starting in their junior year to talk about college preparation and college options. Shen was exposed to a *selective college anywhere* schema in which competitive colleges across the United States were promoted.

For Shen, gaining recognition of these colleges was an important first step in getting him to consider them. In addition to hearing about such colleges from the school, he also relied on other sources of information. This included taking into account the colleges attended by past students and the college recruiters that visited his high school. Despite having never traveled outside California, he was able to evaluate such out-of-state colleges positively. For one, knowing that alumni have attended some of the out-of-state liberal arts colleges gave him a sense of comfort in that if they enjoyed it, he could expect the same. Here he describes the experience of learning about colleges from his school and alumni:

> SHEN: At exposing me to colleges, the school was very helpful because Northside Prep is a college-preparatory school. It is supposed to make students go to college. It helped me a lot, not only academically but it gave me exposure to other students that went to college. For example, a graduate of Northside Prep that went to Carleton, I am going to talk to her on the phone about her experience at Carleton. By going to Northside Prep, you have exposure to other students that went to these colleges so if you ever wanted to go to one of these colleges, you could talk to the students that went there.
>
> INTERVIEWER: How helpful was that?
>
> SHEN: It was good. Not only was I able to learn about what Carleton is like, I was able to learn about their experiences at Carleton and how they enjoyed being at a liberal arts college. So the people at Northside Prep are very helpful in guiding you toward a college that fits best for you.

In addition to knowing that alumni have attended out-of-state liberal arts colleges, he was also attracted to such colleges because of their generous financial aid packages for low-income students, something he learned about from the financial aid night at his high school. This critical piece of information regarding the advertised cost of the college and what students actually pay based on their family's economic situation was something not clearly communicated to other lower-SES students, especially those whose organizational schemas ignored out-of-state or highly selective private universities. Shen ended up applying to two CSUs, four UCs, an in-state private university, and multiple out-of-state liberal arts colleges that included Carleton, Vassar, Wesleyan, and Swarthmore. Shen's experiences at Northside Prep played an important role in his decision to apply to out-of-state liberal arts colleges. In the quote that follows, he discusses why he thought low-income students rarely applied to top colleges across the country and how he himself was able to overcome some of those self-doubts:

> SHEN: It's probably because they are scared to. You don't know because you are low-income. When I was applying to Northside Prep, it was the same thing.

I didn't want to go to a high society school because I would feel like I am different. I want to be with my group of friends. When I was applying to Northside Prep, all the friends that I had made in the past, I had to abandon them to go to Northside Prep.

INTERVIEWER: Do you have the same feeling when you think about applying to these top colleges?

SHEN: Yeah, it's the same feeling but now the experience at Northside Prep, because when I was applying to Northside Prep, my expectations of all my classmates was that that they are all stuck up, rich, and all smart. But that's not the case. Even though I'm low-income, I'm able to do well at this highly competitive school.

Attending Northside Prep forced Shen to give up his neighborhood friends and interact with people from different backgrounds. The experience of having to leave his neighborhood school for a private college preparatory school gave him the confidence to apply to top colleges across the country. His initial fear in applying to out-of-state competitive liberal arts colleges was grounded in doubts about his ability to succeed academically at these top colleges and whether he would fit in socially. Both of these fears were squashed by his successful transition into the private high school. Thus, while his school helped him to recognize out-of-state colleges as appropriate options, it was his favorable experience at the school that led him to evaluate out-of-state colleges positively.

Higher-SES Students

As discussed throughout this book, there are significant divergences in the ways that lower- and higher-SES students understand and act on the idea of attending college in their lives. Prior chapters highlighted the impact of the rationales and framing approaches that students used to understand college attendance and preparation. As discussed in the preceding sections in this chapter, the schemas that lower SES-students were presented with by their high schools and college preparation programs also played a direct role influencing how lower-SES students framed and selected colleges. For higher-SES students, their college-selection processes were also directly influenced by the schemas their schools provided. In contrast to their lower-SES peers, higher-SES students were more likely to pursue admission to prestigious schools out of state.

The higher-SES students in this study attended high schools in which almost all students went on to college. Students at these high schools were presented with a *selective college anywhere* schema in which competitive colleges across the country were framed as appropriate options. This schema of colleges was presented and reinforced by numerous factors, including college presentations at the high school, a history of alumni and peers applying to such colleges, and the suggestions of college counselors. These factors helped to legitimate the schema of colleges that students encountered in their high schools.

All higher-SES students who were interviewed for this book applied to at least one college beyond California. These students' decisions to apply to out-of-state colleges were influenced by multiple key factors. The following sections explain in more detail how each of these different factors was utilized by higher-SES students to make sense of their *selective college anywhere* schema to submit applications to colleges beyond California.

College Rankings

College rankings played a broadly important role for higher-SES students in their college selection, and many higher-SES students consulted college ranking lists to determine where they should submit college applications. Emily, for example, who is Chinese American, was one such student. She attended high school in a community that she described as having a "really good [school] district and it's also very [academically] competitive here." The academic pedigree of the high school was reflected in where students had submitted college applications, which spanned across the country: "Usually [students applied] to the UCs or good private colleges," she noted. "The AP calculus students go to the big UCs, some stay in California, and some of them go to liberal arts colleges. Some go to Ivy League. Colleges like Northeastern, Johns Hopkins, MIT, Stanford."

Though the high school had college counselors available to help students navigate the college exploration process, Emily did not find them helpful. She stated, "We have college counselors, but they don't help you. They only write letters of recommendation." Yet this did not mean that her school did not influence her college choices. It did, but indirectly, by way of the destinations of her high school alumni. Given her perception about the college counselors, Emily took it upon herself to research colleges. She described the process by which she drew on her own preferences and the *selective college anywhere* schema of her school to identify colleges:

INTERVIEWER: Remind me about the criteria that mattered when it came to selecting which college to apply to.

EMILY: It was the rankings. It seems kind of shallow but the rankings actually take into account a lot of criteria which I know someone could argue it's just numbers, it's stupid looking at the rankings. But it [rankings] looks at the quality of the education based on student accounts, quality of professors, SAT scores, GPA. I want to go to competitive schools where people are smart and try hard. Faculty–student ratios, it's all taken into account into the rankings.

INTERVIEWER: What ranking list do you consult?
EMILY: Google. QS World Ranking. US News and Report College. Princeton Review.

As one of the top students at her high school, Emily was not satisfied with getting into a good college. Instead, she actively researched and sought out the very best colleges and universities across the country. Emily also consulted other sources to confirm the experiences of students beyond the ranking lists themselves. She recalled browsing "different search engines, College Board, College Credential, Naviance—our school website, unique student views, Princeton Review, US World Rankings, just all these websites that would give different perspectives and information." In the end, she submitted applications to several UCs, multiple Ivy League universities, and other top out-of-state private research universities and liberal arts colleges.

Lan, another Chinese American student, also drew heavily on college ranking lists to narrow down the *selective college anywhere schema* he was offered via his school. In the following excerpt, Lan discussed the colleges that came to recruit at his high school:

LAN: In the fall, a lot of colleges come to visit, and I started going to them in my junior year and that's when I heard about what they were looking for.
INTERVIEWER: Which colleges usually visit?
LAN: All the UCs. NYU. I don't think any Ivies visited. Michigan. University of Chicago. Puget Sound. Harvey Mudd. Wesleyan. They are mostly middle- to upper-tiered colleges. The very top colleges, I don't think they come out here. I don't know why.

While any college was possible for students attending his school, Lan recounted how he drew heavily on college ranking lists to narrow down his option: "I started doing research the summer before senior year. That's when I made a spreadsheet of different colleges that I thought I would like. I used the rankings, US News. . . . I took the top twenty, top thirty schools, and put them down in the spreadsheet." Lan narrowed his list further by emphasizing colleges on the East Coast that are close to a major city with opportunities for internships and jobs. While he did not initially consider small liberal arts colleges, the positive experience of a friend at such a college convinced him to do more research on it:

Somewhere in the process, one of my friends said you should look into the smaller schools and so I did. I researched Amherst, Swarthmore, Pomona, Wesleyan. Our school uses Naviance; it's a service that you can send them your transcripts, letters of recommendations, [and] they have a college search option so I put in what I wanted. They have twenty different criteria, and they showed me a bunch of results. Some of them matched 100 percent of the results. Those were Williams, Amherst, Swarthmore, Yale so I came up with a pretty big list and started narrowing them down.

Thus his high school influenced his choices of college through his peer and the college search program. Lan ultimately submitted applications to the UCs, Ivy League universities, both in-state and out-of-state private research universities, and liberal arts colleges. For higher-SES students like Lan, college rankings helped them refine and narrow their choices. The *selective colleges anywhere* schema enabled them to view colleges across the country as appropriate options, but their desire to enter the top colleges required that they do their own research to identify the very top colleges. This approach stands in contrast to those of lower-SES students, including those students who were exposed to a *selective college anywhere* schema. Lower-SES students rarely brought up the use of college ranking lists in their selection of colleges. This may not be surprising given chapter 2's examination of social class differences in the college preparation approaches of students. Given that higher-SES students framed college preparation as standing out among other competitive applicants, their choices of colleges can be seen as reflective of their need to get into the most prestigious colleges as a way to distinguish themselves from other students.

Small Colleges

Another important factor for higher-SES students was the size of the school. Most higher-SES students preferred smaller private universities, specifically liberal arts colleges, due to the exposure to such colleges in high school and because of the perceived more intimate academic learning environments of these institutions. Macy, a white student, was one such student who prioritized applying to liberal arts colleges. In recounting the college destinations of former students and the type of college recruiters that visit their campus, Macy described a *selective college anywhere* schema of colleges:

INTERVIEWER: What schools actually recruit at Franklin High?

MACY: So many. Northwestern. Just a huge range. Bucknell, Villanova. Trying to think of the ones that I went to. Some from Ohio. NYU. I don't know. All those huge range of schools, a lot of very good schools. A lot of the UCs. I didn't go to the UC ones. . . . A lot of UPenn, Amherst, Middlebury. Hamilton. Those kinds of schools. A lot of liberal arts schools. A lot of people from Franklin go to liberal arts schools. I think it's because we go to a small school, and a lot of kids feel comfortable at small schools. I know that a lot of people apply to Michigan and Wisconsin, those big academic schools. A lot of these schools also come and recruit. Just a lot of schools like that. Duke. Tulane.

Macy's school exposed her to a wide variety of competitive colleges. When asked how she gathered information about which colleges she would apply to, she referenced the college presentations: "All those schools that came to our school to give presentations at my school. A lot of people from Franklin High School go to those schools." Liberal arts colleges, which have small student populations, are popular among students at her school because they resemble the experience that students have in their small high school. Macy's interest in liberal arts colleges shaped how she approached the college exploration and application process. Many liberal arts colleges are located outside California. Thus she made it a priority to apply to schools outside California:

INTERVIEWER: There are so many colleges. What process did you go through to narrow down to a list?

MACY: I don't want to go to school in the South so I crossed them out. I didn't really want to go to school in California but I applied to UC Davis but I canceled that now that I am not going there. I wanted to experience something new for four years. Get a change of pace. Get a fun, new, cool experience. I was looking at school on the West Coast, Midwest. I didn't really want to go to a huge school. A middle or smaller school, a midsize school is my ideal one. Softball, I was thinking I want to play softball, which is mostly at a small school, and I don't really mind that. That's how I narrowed it down.

INTERVIEWER: You mostly looked at the small schools?

MACY: I just like hear about people going to Cal [UC Berkeley] and being in a 500 [student] class taught by a TA. Sometimes I have trouble paying attention. I like to space out so I just don't think I will be able to focus in those classes. I like to create relationships with my teachers and use them as resources. You can really do that at small colleges. You can't really do that at larger schools.

Macy's experience at her high school shaped her interest in out-of-state colleges, specifically liberal arts colleges. She attended a small high school and sought out colleges that possessed some of the qualities of a small institution. She found these qualities primarily in liberal arts colleges, institutions that have a prominent profile at her school because of their recruitment visits and the large number of alumni that have attended these colleges. In the end, she applied to one small, in-state private college, one out-of-state public university, an out-of-state private research university, and eight out-of-state liberal arts colleges.

The importance of small class sizes and more intimate connections with faculty were also emphasized by other students. Sophie, a white student, emphasized this as a major attraction of private and liberal arts colleges. She noted, "I wanted to go somewhere where I can get to know my professors. Smaller classes and discussions." Similarly, Yuna, a Japanese American student, was concerned about the problem of overcrowding at public universities and so she specifically sought out smaller private universities: "I like how it is easier to get classes if you are in the private schools because there are so many people in public schools and they can't really take care of you. It's a battlefield and you choose class and some people stay there for six years because they can't get their classes. The same with state schools. That worries me a little bit."

Both Sophie and Yuna ended up applying to large public universities, such as the UCs, private research universities, and multiple liberal arts colleges. Their preference for and applications to relatively small colleges in the form of liberal arts colleges are not just a function of exposure to these colleges. Instead, their experiences in a small school and their connections to alumni who have attended different types of colleges gave them insights that made school size a meaningful criterion in their selection of colleges. In the case of their lower-SES counterparts, who were also informed about such colleges but did not submit application to such colleges, it can be seen how the absence of experience in a small high school or the lack of understanding about the benefits and drawbacks to colleges of different population size can be a barrier to applying to liberal arts colleges.

Large Universities

Although most higher-SES students who were interviewed for this book were interested in smaller colleges, this was not universal, and some higher-SES students preferred large college campuses as a way to experience a different educational environment. This preference among some higher SES students for larger campuses overlapped more with the preferences of lower-SES students who also generally preferred large schools. However, the reasons among the different groups for choosing larger universities often differed—with lower-SES students homing in on the diversity at larger universities and their concerns about fitting in at smaller colleges, while higher-SES students tended to focus on academics and educational experience. Scott, for example, a multiracial student, was one of these higher-SES students who actually preferred larger colleges. He attended a relatively small high school with about two hundred students in each grade. In a school in which college attendance was an accepted fact, there was immense expectation for students to do well. The condition of the school, characterized by its competitive nature and the inevitability of college after high school, influenced the configuration of colleges that students were exposed to via their high school. Counselors met individually with students to help them identify colleges from a *selective college anywhere* schema. Scott revealed how no college was beyond the reach of students at the school: "It's all over the place. For my journalism class, we make a map of where everyone goes, and the pins are across the board."

While there were no geographic boundaries as to where students can go for college, there was a common understanding among the students regarding certain types of colleges that were considered inferior and thus should be avoided. Lower-ranked colleges and universities were shunned while top ranked institutions were viewed as highly desirable. The result was a shared understanding of appropriate colleges based on the prestige and reputation of the colleges.

Scott drew from this shared understanding of appropriate options to make his decision about where to apply to college. In evaluating which colleges constituted a right fit for him, Scott relied on his experiences and preferences to narrow the realm of potential colleges. Having grown up in a small community and attended a small high school, Scott wanted a larger school where he could meet more people and be given more independence:

> SCOTT: All the schools I applied to with the exception of Reed, I think they are all over 20,000 students. Obviously they are big. After that, it's just so obvious. Boston [University] and NYU, they host you overnight. They have a whole program for an entire weekend. "Oh, look at us, we really want you to be here." The public schools are more like, "You can come here." They are much more self-motivated. They are much more like UWash [University of Washington], UCSC [University of California, Santa Cruz], "You can come here." They don't need you to come.
>
> INTERVIEWER: You prefer one approach over the other?
>
> SCOTT: As much as the handholding is as easy as they make things, for the hands-off, that's just more realistic for life. I don't need high school again where your teachers are asking you about how your project is going. It's interactive. I'd rather just do it my own way.

As the foregoing exchange demonstrated, Scott understood larger schools as giving students more flexibility but also strengthening students' discipline, something he felt was lacking at smaller campuses. He believed larger schools would provide him with the skills to navigate life after college. This understanding, based on his experience in high school and some college visits, played an important role in his evaluation of what colleges were right for him. He also wanted to be far away from home: "With the exception of Berkeley, I wanted to get away from the Bay Area." In the end, Scott applied to one CSU, multiple UCs, an in-state private university, and several out-of-state public and private research universities. The example of Scott demonstrates how the factors that motivate higher-SES students to seek out larger college campuses differ from those of their lower-SES peers. Whereas lower-SES students tended to focus on social belonging on college campuses given their lower-SES and nonwhite status, choices of higher-SES students were driven more by what they saw as the fit between the skills they wanted to develop and the type of student dispositions that colleges foster.

Location Away from Home

Like their lower-SES peers, location was also an important criterion in where higher-SES students applied to college. However, there was a major difference in the way students utilized this preference for selecting colleges. In contrast to lower-SES students, most higher-SES students preferred colleges located far from home. Nick, a white student, was someone who made sense of the *selective college anywhere* schema by focusing his efforts on applying to colleges beyond California. While he submitted applications to the UCs, he was set on attending a private college outside California. He stated, "I was much more focused on private schools. I imagine myself moving out of California and getting new experiences and perspective. And the most logical way to do that was to go to a private and not a public school."

Nick's emphasis on private colleges outside California was shaped by his interest in following in the footsteps of his older brother. Nick accompanied his mother and brother to visit colleges when his brother was applying to colleges. His brother ultimately attended a school in the Midwest. Based on these college trips and conversations with his brother about life in the Midwest, Nick was intent on attending college outside California: "Getting away from California. I love California. I can imagine moving back when I'm older. So many things to see and weather's great. At the same time, I visited other places in the United States, I really want to be in a different place and get a truly different perspective outside of just being on a campus. People in California, once you come here, you don't want to leave. You are like in a bubble. I thought the best way to really challenge my view is to go somewhere else."

Although he did apply to several UCs, his desire to remove himself from the bubble of California led him to submit applications to multiple Ivy Leagues, some liberal arts colleges, and some research universities in the Midwest.

Other higher-SES students also prioritized colleges outside California for similar reasons. Here Mary, a Chinese American student, discussed her reasoning:

MARY: I would like to be far away from home. I like to go to college on the East Coast for undergrad and come back to California to live or something.

INTERVIEWER: Tell me more about your interest in the East Coast?

MARY: I feel like it's important to have a different experience in a different atmosphere at one point in your life. I want to live here because of the weather. It's California. I'm thinking it'd be nice to move there for four years and then move back.

INTERVIEWER: Some students are apprehensive about going far, what makes you embrace being far away from home?

MARY: My personality. I like to do things on my own. I like the challenge just to see if I can live on my own. If I go to UCB [UC Berkeley], my parents are next to it.

Even the few higher-SES students who stated their intention of staying close to home still applied to out-of-state colleges (although their choices were limited to colleges in the region), revealing the powerful influence that the *selective college anywhere* schema has on the decision-making process of higher-SES students. Daisy, a white student, was among the few who preferred colleges close to home. While recognizing that any college was possible for students at her high school, she engaged in her own evaluation to decide which ones were the right fit. Daisy preferred to stay as close to California as possible: "Some people stay in California and some people don't. There's no particular focus on staying local or on leaving. It's like every person's preference. I know I want to stay close because I have issues with being in the wild unknown. . . . I generally want to stay in state. . . . It had to be in or near California or be very impressive."

Unlike lower-SES students who rejected out-of-state colleges because they had never traveled outside California, Daisy had visited some places but was not particularly fond of them. As someone who admitted to being shy, Daisy felt overwhelmed in the presence of large numbers of strangers. Yet she still applied to an out-of-state college in Oregon: "It's in Oregon, it's the furthest away from home that I applied." Other students at her school had been admitted there in the past, which made it less intimidating even though it is outside California. In the end, Daisy applied to several UCs, one CSU, one in-state liberal arts college, and the Oregon liberal arts college. Although she selected different universities than Mary and Nick, Daisy's case further highlights the importance of schemas. Schemas include not just exposure to information about colleges but also knowledge that past students have attended such colleges, which makes these places less daunting as academic or social transitions.

Conclusion

For both lower-SES students and higher-SES students, high schools and college preparation programs do not simply provide information about colleges. A more apt characterization would be that high schools and programs are organizations that socialize students to have preferences for some higher education institutions over others. For the scores of students interviewed for this book, this socialization process took place via multiple actors within the school and program settings, including teachers, counselors, program staff, peers, and postsecondary education recruiters. The decision on where to submit college applications thus represented the culmination of years of socialization in these organizational settings.

Higher-SES students attended high schools in which competitive and highly ranked colleges in California and across the country were viewed as appropriate options. Like other students from affluent communities and schools, they were prepared for and encouraged to submit applications to the top colleges (Mullen 2009). These students benefited from a high school culture that emphasized these colleges and a recruiting environment that favored students like them. Admissions officers from selective colleges tend to concentrate their visits to schools and communities that have many students with the academic preparation and social backgrounds that make them likely applicants (Zemsky and Oedel 1983; Avery and Levin 2009). Such colleges tend to recruit in areas close to where they are located and in large urban areas with high concentrations of high-achieving students. As a result, students in such areas are more likely to be exposed to elite colleges, helping them cultivate a desire to attend a highly selective institution (Hill and Winston 2006 Hoxby and Avery 2012; Radford 2013). Not surprisingly, applications to out-of-state colleges were a common occurrence among higher-SES students in this study.

In contrast, most lower-SES students attended high schools and participated in college preparation programs that only presented them with colleges in California. Research has demonstrated that high schools with large concentrations of low-income students lack the resources typically available in schools with higher-income students (Perna 2008; Radford 2013). As a result, students from public and low-income schools are at a disadvantage when it comes to getting exposure to a spectrum of college options. The lack of college exposure to a wide array of colleges is especially harmful to high-achieving students who have the qualifications to compete for admission into the top colleges across the United States. Radford (2013) attributes the lack of information about private selective colleges to the high schools' efforts to cater their college exploration to the average students rather than the top students. Similarly, Perna (2008) finds that resource constraints in public and low-income schools shift the focus of counseling to the needs of the schools' average or neediest students, which typically revolve around satisfying requirements for graduation. Serving the needs of the average students often results in fewer college-related services for college-bound students. Consequently, high-achieving students often do not get the resources and guidance they need to apply to more selective universities and colleges.

Some lower-SES students, specifically those in better resourced schools and those in programs geared toward getting high-achieving students into the top colleges across the country, were more likely to be exposed to a schema of colleges that included out-of-state colleges. However, being presented with a configuration of colleges that included out-of-state colleges was often not enough to get some lower-SES students to submit applications to those colleges. Lower-SES students who did apply to out-of-state colleges tended to have experiences in out-of-state environments or positive experiences with higher-SES students in better resourced high schools. These experiences were instrumental in shaping their desire to apply to out-of-state colleges.

Organizations such as high schools and college preparation programs shaped the college choices of students by imposing boundaries around which types of colleges the organizations considered appropriate for their students. These organizations did this by providing students with socially shared schemas to make sense of the available options after high school. Schemas helped students narrow down the multitude of options to a manageable set. In schools in which few students go on to attend four-year colleges, such as lower-SES schools, students were exposed to a greater variety of post–high school options. This consisted of in-state two-year and four-year colleges, and to a lesser extent vocational schools in close proximity to the high school. In high schools in which most students were expected to matriculate to four-year colleges, such as higher-SES schools, students were exposed to schemas of four-year competitive colleges across the country, ranging from small private liberal arts colleges to large public universities.

The same mechanism operated within college preparation programs for lower-SES students. The majority of college preparation programs, also known as early intervention programs or pre-college outreach programs, are designed to prepare low-income students for postsecondary attendance and success (Swail and Perna 2002; Villalpando and Solarzano 2005; Seftor, Mamun, and Schirm 2009). In a study of one of the largest college outreach programs, Neil Seftor and colleagues (2009) found that when compared to other highly motivated students from disadvantaged backgrounds not enrolled in the program, the students who participated in this program had higher rates of postsecondary enrollment and completion. However, participation did not significantly affect the type or selectivity of postsecondary institutions attended by eligible applicants. Similarly, among all the students interviewed for this book (who were all from California), general college preparation programs primarily exposed them to public four-year colleges in California. In contrast, programs that specifically enrolled higher-achieving students emphasized schemas of colleges that consisted of competitive colleges across the country.

While high schools and college preparation programs imposed boundaries around which options were appropriate and therefore acceptable, students themselves exercised some level of agency in choosing what options were the right fit for them. Distinguishing between appropriate and right options recognizes that the schemas of organizations are mediated by each individual's understandings, experiences, and preferences. Students were not merely passive recipients of the configuration of options that were transmitted to them from their schools or college preparation programs. Instead, they were agents who also tried to make sense of these appropriate options based on the experiences and understandings they brought to the decision-making process. Although students exercised agency in choosing the colleges that were the right fit for them, it was a restricted agency. Students were choosing—but based on a set of confined choices set by the institutions.

High schools and college preparation programs matter in the college choice decision-making process for more than just their ability to provide information. Among lower-SES students, information was a necessary but insufficient condition for application to certain types of colleges, specifically out-of-state colleges. Thus explanations that rely exclusively on information overlook how the context in which the information was received interacts with the understandings and experiences that students bring to the college choice decision-making process.

The inadequacy of information-only explanations can be seen in the examples of the lower-SES students who were exposed to colleges beyond California but did not submit an application to such colleges. These students had information about higher education institutions, such as small liberal arts colleges and elite private universities, but they did not find such places desirable given their background and experiences. Even higher-SES students, all of whom submitted applications to at least an out-of-state college, had access to more than just information about such institutions. Their decision to submit applications to out-of-state colleges was influenced by the fact that previous students from their high schools and communities had successfully matriculated to these institutions. Many higher-SES students thus had personal connections to individuals in such colleges. These personal connections were essential in shaping their desire to attend these types of colleges.

Social class background certainly shaped access to the quality of the high schools and consequently the types of colleges to which students were exposed. Yet this does not mean that only social class differences matter in explaining where students submit college applications. Beyond social class, race also shaped the colleges to which students were exposed. Among lower-SES students, Asian American students were more likely to be enrolled in high schools and college preparation programs that exposed them to a *selective college anywhere* schema, which made them more likely to apply to top colleges outside California. This was due largely to the fact that Asian American students were more likely than their Black and Hispanic peers to attend better quality high schools and participate in college preparation programs that actively sought to get their students into small liberal arts colleges and private universities, many of which are outside California.

Race also influenced how students think about their fit at colleges and universities. Many lower-SES students across all racial groups were worried about the social and cultural challenges that exist in pursuing higher education beyond California. However, the fact that the student demographics of private universities beyond California are predominantly white or white and Asian presented an additional barrier to non-Asian minority students. For Black and Hispanic students who were thinking about submitting applications to top colleges beyond California, it was not simply about adjusting to a new and different environment. It was also about racial inclusion, the ability to see oneself represented at these institutions and to feel that there is a community of people with similar racial backgrounds and experiences.

These patterns of decision making among both higher- and lower-SES students reveal many of the intersecting factors that drive student application and attendance trends, while also highlighting important areas of potential intervention for educators and policy makers hoping to reduce the larger admission gaps between lower- and higher-SES students at top colleges. To increase the college application rates of lower-SES students to the nation's top colleges and universities, it is important to keep in mind that information is important but often insufficient. Students need to be able to make sense of information that they receive about colleges in a way that makes those colleges personally appealing to them. The context under which students receive that information and the life experiences that students draw on to interpret that information are critical components to the decision-making process. A higher-SES student learning about small liberal arts colleges or Ivy League universities from their high schools and alumni does so within a context that is distinctly different from that of a lower-SES student who is introduced to it through a program. Moreover, higher-SES students are prioritizing colleges that are far from home and those that are high on college ranking lists, factors typically not significant to the college searches of lower-SES students. Lower-SES students can find these top colleges appealing if information about these top colleges is presented in a context that takes into account what is meaningful to them and if they are provided experiences that can help them rationalize the benefits of these top colleges, many of which are located far from home.

4

Narratives of Interdependence and Independence

• • • • • • • • • • • • • • • • • • • •

> I only applied to colleges in California. Only Stanford [is private], the rest are California public schools. I know it'll be closer and in a sense easier to help my mom than out of state. (Jack, lower-SES Chinese American student)

> I didn't think about it as I'm going away from home. It's like I'm just going someplace different. . . . I have absolutely no problem going to school there [far away]. I want to go on adventures. I want to experience the world. That means I have to leave California. I love traveling to new places so I'll be fine. (Anna, higher-SES white student)

In the quotes above, two students—one from a family of a lower socioeconomic status, and the other from a family of a higher socioeconomic status—present two very different explanations for their decisions to submit applications to colleges beyond California. Jack, the lower-SES student, suggests he did not apply to any colleges beyond California due in large part to his concern about the well-being of his immigrant mother whom he had been looking after throughout high school. For Anna, the higher-SES student, pursuing colleges beyond California represented an opportunity for her to be exposed to a new set of experiences. Due to their social class backgrounds, they each understood college differently, and this meaning shaped where they applied to college.

Chapter 3 examined how the schemas of colleges that students obtained from organizations like their high schools and college preparation programs interacted with their own preferences and considerations to shape where they submitted college applications. This chapter delves more deeply into a key criterion—distance from home—a criterion which both groups of students utilized in their college choice decision-making process. Whereas organizations shaped the types of colleges to which students were exposed, family upbringing and experiences were important influences for how far from home students thought they could go for college.

For all students, the decision about where they should spend the next four-plus years of their life after high school was not just a personal matter; it involved more than merely evaluating the characteristics of the available college options. The decision was as personal and individual as it was familial and social. In other words, the college choice decision-making process was deeply embedded within the socialization experiences of the family. The family represented an important factor in shaping the college preferences of students in notable ways. Families exerted direct influences on the college choices of students through the suggestions of specific colleges that students ought to pursue. Parents and older siblings conveyed to college-bound students the types of colleges and universities they believed were most appropriate for students. Depending on their family background, some students encountered college recommendations throughout their childhood into high school. Others found out what colleges their family considered acceptable only when they started the application process.

Beyond college recommendations, families also shaped the college choices of students indirectly via the experiences that students accumulated outside school. What students saw and encountered at home and the type of experiences that parents were able to provide to their children were consequential to how students made sense of higher education. These indirect influences on students' college choices did not necessarily involve colleges, but they had a lasting impact on students' decisions as they drew on such experiences to think about where to submit college applications. These indirect influences of the families are the primary focus of this chapter.

Through the concept of narratives, I show the specific aspects of family experiences and upbringing that matter and how they matter in the decision-making process. Narratives reflect the stories that individuals tell to express how they make sense of their lives (Somers 1994; Lamont and Small 2008). Narratives represent the events that students deem meaningful—encounters and experiences that students believe explain whom they are and where they are headed. While they are interpretations, they are powerful because these perceptions come to shape how students think about their future. Narratives influence decision making and behaviors because individuals choose actions that are consistent with their personal narratives (Somers 1994). As such, the concept of narratives shows how the stories students present regarding how they understand their relationship to their family have a significant impact on what colleges they frame as reflecting whom they are and whom they want to become.

I show that part of the explanation for social class differences in application to out-of-state colleges can be found in how much autonomy students perceived they had over their decision making. When discussing their decision-making processes, higher-SES students presented a narrative of independence regarding what they had done to prepare for college and where they would apply. They emphasized aspects of their upbringing and experiences that demonstrated how they exercised initiative in making decisions about what activities they would participate in. They downplayed the influence of their parents in making these decisions, and they saw themselves as individuals who are autonomous in choosing their directions and college options.

In contrast, lower-SES students spoke of experiences and considerations that reflected a narrative of interdependence between themselves and their parents that was grounded in the mutual concern that they had for one another as the prospect of college loomed. Lower-SES students recognized the struggles their parents had to overcome and they developed a sense of responsibility for their parents. Some students had assumed family responsibilities throughout high school. Others had parents who pressed them to consider attending only those colleges near home. These factors reinforced a narrative of interdependence that the fate of students and parents was intertwined.

As a result, higher-SES students framed college as an opportunity to leave their families and immerse themselves in an environment far from home, whereas lower-SES students understood college as a continuation of family interdependence. Consequently, higher-SES students were more likely to apply to selective private universities in other parts of the country, whereas lower-SES students tended to limit their choices to selective and nonselective colleges closer to home.

Narratives of Interdependence among Lower-SES Students

Among the nearly two dozen lower-SES students that were interviewed for this book, many recounted stories that reflected narratives of interdependence. These stories included students' awareness of the sacrifices and struggles of their parents to support the family, students' family responsibilities while in high school, students' anticipation of their role in the health and success of their family in the future, and parental pressures for students to stay close to home for college. While not all of these themes came up for every student, some combination of them emerged in many lower-SES students' discussions about their upbringings and experiences. Variations in the narratives of interdependence as expressed by the different themes corresponded to differences in social backgrounds, such as gender, immigrant background, and race.

Due to these narratives of interdependence, lower-SES students recognized the importance of mutual support between themselves and their parents in any future success. Consequently, these students viewed making decisions about college as requiring consideration of the real and perceived needs and wishes of the family. This understanding imposed geographic constraints on many lower-SES students such that they viewed only colleges close to home and specifically those in California as viable options.

Research has demonstrated that a strong obligation to assist the family such as those reflected in the narratives of interdependence among lower-SES students in this study can involve responsibilities and activities that compromise the ability of young adults to pursue postsecondary schooling (Fuligni and Pedersen 2002; Desmond and Lopez Turley 2009). Matthew Desmond and Ruth Lopez Turley (2009) find that a cultural preference privileging family goals over individual goals, which they term familism, discourages some Latino/a youth from applying to selective colleges if they must leave home. According to Sarah Ovink and Demetra Kalogrides (2015), familism is not just a Latino/a phenomenon but one that is shared by students from disadvantaged backgrounds more generally. The lower-SES students interviewed for this study discussed family relationships that reflected this kind of familism—maintaining family ties was an important consideration among poor and working-class students, making it difficult for students to seriously consider out-of-state colleges or to take advantage of academic opportunities located far from home (Stuber 2009; Mullen 2011; Lee and Kramer 2013). Next I examine the different elements of lower-SES students' narrative of interdependence.

Interdependence Grounded in Immediate and Anticipatory Family Obligations

One of the ways in which family experiences constrained the college choices of lower-SES students was through the impact that immediate family obligations had on students' anticipation of having to fulfill these obligations in the future. This anticipation had the effect of restricting how far from home students thought they could attend college. These lower-SES students had to contend with family responsibilities while in high school, and they drew on such obligations to make sense of the college choice decision-making process. The students who felt this way were most often children of Asian immigrants whose parents spoke very little English. They often served as interpreters for their parents and mediated interactions with professionals and institutions. As they pondered their future, these students worried about their ability to fulfill these responsibilities while away in college. Jack, the son and only child of Chinese immigrants, was among the students whose upbringing and family experiences reflected a narrative grounded in immediate and anticipatory family obligations. His father passed away during his junior year in high school, and his mother worked around the clock as an in-home caregiver. As a consequence, Jack carried on many responsibilities on behalf of his mother. This theme of having to intervene on behalf of his mother continued throughout high school. While he viewed these responsibilities as an inconvenience, he understood that they were something he must do for his mother:

> JACK: Yeah, I really don't like it [family responsibilities]. I know it's partially my responsibility to help her because, as her son, she's helped me as a mother. . . . I help my mom to relieve this guilt of having to take care of me. She works so much and for so long and I respect her for that. I understand it's all for me. I don't like to but I do my best to help her.
>
> INTERVIEWER: Knowing that, how does it make you feel about your own life?
>
> JACK: It gives me guilt because she's working very hard as an immigrant [and she] doesn't understand English. She's working really hard to support us. I know that she relies on me a lot. Honestly, it is still a major issue weighing on me. What will she do if I go to college? She wants me to go to college. I want to go to college. The issue is I don't know when I go to college, what will happen to her when she needs me. What if there's important mail or information like legal crap and she doesn't have anyone except me and I'm miles away?

Jack recognized the sacrifices his mother has made for him. Knowing this, he felt obligated to support his mother as much as he could. This sense of obligation and the accompanying guilt shaped how Jack thought about his future. The prioritization of his mother's needs in his decision about college is demonstrated in the following exchange when Jack reflected on the implications of his family responsibilities for his college and career trajectory:

> JACK: That's the reason why I didn't apply to colleges out of state. I only applied to colleges in California. Only Stanford, the rest are California public schools. I know it'll be closer and in a sense easier to help my mom than out of state.
>
> INTERVIEWER: Outside of California, [is it] harder to help your mom?
>
> JACK: Yeah, in state, I feel like I'll have a few good friends who will allow me to borrow money or drive me back to help my mom out for a bit. Worse comes to worst, I always have this surplus amount of money to buy a ticket home. Out of state is not an option and a plane ticket is not an option. I'm going to college for economic reasons.

Jack felt constrained in his decision-making regarding where he can attend college. For Jack, college meant a continuance of family responsibilities and the possibility that he may be called on to assist his mother. This sense of obligation was further exacerbated by his family's low-income background. Knowing that he would likely need to come home at a moment's notice, he worried about his ability to do so given his family's limited economic means. In anticipation of these difficulties, Jack planned to save up an emergency fund and to rely on his college friends for assistance. To make college work for both him and his mother, Jack needed to strike a balance between going to a good college and one that he can get home from affordably. This was accomplished by limiting his choices to colleges in California. Jack submitted applications to five UCs, four CSUs, and Stanford, all colleges in California.

Meiying, the daughter of Chinese immigrants, was another student who had to support her family while in high school. She also projected these responsibilities onto the future. During her junior year in high school, her mother developed an injury at work. Meiying accompanied her mother to many of her doctor visits. At the time of the interview, her mother had traveled abroad to seek additional treatment. In the absence of her mother, Meiying took on additional family responsibilities while her father worked to support the family. Her list of responsibilities included driving her brother to school, shopping for the family, and performing household chores. These responsibilities have caused her to occasionally question the prospect of attending college away from home: "I don't know how I feel about going away from home. I do hope that my mom gets better after she comes back. I have been taking care of her and my brother this year so if I go away next year, I guess my mom would have to take care of my brother or he'll have to take care of himself. . . . I don't know how my brother will take care of himself. Even though he's one year younger, I do most of the housework. He doesn't really do much around the house."

Unlike Jack, Meiying also had to contend with the fact that her parents insisted that she stay close to home for college, a common theme, especially among lower-SES female students:

MEIYING: They want me to stay local. They want me to stay close to home so like [UC] Berkeley. But I actually like [UC] LA better than [UC] Berkeley. I guess it comes down to financial packages. They tell me straight up, "If you get accepted to [UC] LA and [UC] Berkeley, you are going to go to [UC] Berkeley." And then my mom said she'll bring me food every single week so they still want to take care of me.

INTERVIEWER: Stay close to provide you food or something else?

MEIYING: Since they are very protective of me, they always make sure that I am safe. I think they want to continue looking after me in college. If I go far away to college and something happens, they can't get to me because they don't speak English, and they don't know how to communicate with people around them. I think it's better for me to be around them and help them when they need help.

Meiying's responsibilities as a daughter and the oldest child in her working class, immigrant family added additional layers of consideration to where she could go to college. Like Jack, Meiying projected what family life would be like in her absence when she is in college. Given the centrality of Meiying's role in her family, she had to take into account the needs of her family. On top of these responsibilities, she was faced with parents who are reluctant to let her attend college far from home. As a result, she viewed college as a continuance of the family–child interdependence that has followed her throughout high school. This narrative of interdependence imposed limitations on her choices of colleges, forcing her to consider only colleges in California. She ended up applying to four UCs, four CSUs, and some private universities.

Interdependence Grounded in Anticipatory Family Concerns

Another way in which family experiences constrained students' college choices was in the way students anticipated family crises and the impact it had on how they thought about their role and responsibilities to such crises. Most lower-SES students did not have to actively support or intervene on their parents' behalf while they were in high school. Even with little to no current family obligations, these students still felt tied to their parents' well-being, and they worried about their family as they looked toward their future. One such student was Carlos, the son of Mexican immigrants. He lived with his father and two older brothers. His father was employed as a construction worker, and one of Carlos's motivations for going to college came from recognizing the grueling nature of his father's job: "From my perspective," Carlos said, "I should actually get my dad out of what he's doing to get him a better life."

While Carlos was committed to becoming the first person in his family to graduate from college, he had concerns about what that journey entailed for his family. He did not have family responsibilities, but he depended on his father for moral and social support. Moreover, he was concerned about his father's health. This narrative of interdependence, the belief that children and their parents are connected to the well-being and success of one another, factored into Carlos's thought process about where he should attend college.

CARLOS: I told my dad that I applied to [UC] LA. He told me "LA? Why LA." I feel like my dad wants me to stay close. He doesn't want me to go far. It would be the same with my mom. At the end of the day, it's up to me. I'm pretty sure my dad is going to understand what I'm going to do.

INTERVIEWER: What does your dad say that tells you he wants you to stay close to home?

CARLOS: I don't know. The things that my dad does. I feel if I go far away, I'm going to miss my dad. I'm going to miss what he does. My dad cooks. I'm going to miss my dad's food. I'm going to miss the presence of my dad. Me and my dad, we always laugh so I feel like those jokes and laughter I'm going to miss a lot. And then with his job, I don't know [if] at the end of the day, when I go back home from school I'm never certain if he's alive or something bad happened. When I go to college, I won't know until I call him when he comes home. I'm kind of scared because I never know if my dad's okay.

Carlos, like any student on the cusp of college, dreaded what he would miss about home when he has to leave for college. He also confronted a set of challenges that reflected his working class, immigrant background. His father was employed in a physically demanding occupation that put him at a higher risk of injury, something that worried Carlos. Moreover, Carlos also had to contend with the reality that his parents face restrictions in where they can travel because of their immigration status. He states, "I've always been in Richmond. My parents not having documents or papers, we can't really travel outside of California." Carlos's decision about where he could attend college was saturated with multiple constraints. He gave little consideration to colleges beyond California and ended up applying to four UCs and four CSUs in California.

Marcus, the son of an African American couple, was another student who worried about his family when he thought about the prospect of college. Both of his parents briefly attended college but neither finished. Born and raised in the South, he and his family relocated multiple times across the country in search of more stable employment. At one time, they were homeless for several months. These experiences shaped how he thought about the importance of his family: "We are close because, my parents, they only have a high school degree and they are always working. Me and my brothers, we are close because we don't have anyone to depend on. We move around too much so we need each other. We depend on each other because my parents are always working. We developed a tight-knit relationship with each other. I say we are pretty close."

The importance of maintaining ties with family members was also reinforced explicitly by his parents, who attributed their precarious living situation to the lack of strong bonds with their extended family: "I think the biggest thing that they [my parents] have tried to enforce is that when we get our own family is to make sure that we become close to our relatives because they are saying that having access to relatives and getting to know them would have helped us on multiple occasions. We wouldn't have had to move so much if we had relatives help us out in certain situations. Because we didn't have that, we had to move where we could to find money."

This experience with poverty, displacement, and reliance on one's family deeply affected how Marcus thought about college. As someone interested in studying engineering, with an emphasis on robotics, he was well aware of the importance of going to a school that specialized in that field. However, his family upbringing and experiences sprinkled doubts on where he could attend college. His family recently moved to the Bay Area to be closer to their extended family. But even here, he continued to be troubled by family issues. He reflected on his decision against applying to out-of-state colleges, specifically to his dream school of the Massachusetts Institute of Technology (MIT):

MARCUS: At the moment, I'm more keen on going to a UC because of all the deaths or things in my family. I still want to go to MIT, it's still my number one choice but I have to put that aside for when I go for my graduate degree. At the moment, I'm going to try to stay in state.

INTERVIEWER: You say you want to stay close to home. Tell me more about that.

MARCUS: As I stated earlier, there's been a whole bunch of deaths in my family. My grandpa died about two months prior and my grandma died yesterday. My uncle has stage four cancer, and he's going to die soon. And so then, I want to be there to support them. As of now, my studies have to come first. The things I want to do like getting my little brother to go to college, it's not going to give him a good reason to go if I don't finish.

INTERVIEWER: What kind of support do you anticipate providing if you stay in California versus being on the East Coast?

MARCUS: As of now, I don't think there's much I can offer or do. Or wait for times to heal their wounds. Right now, I think I feel it's better for me to be in the vicinity to help out than leave.

Despite the countless obstacles and issues that he and his family has endured, Marcus remained steadfast in his commitment to attend college. However, his family experiences and the anticipation of family struggles forced him to push off more ambitious goals like attending MIT. His narrative of interdependence, expressed in his awareness of the importance of a close-knit family for overcoming crises, grounded his decision to apply only to colleges in California. He applied to four UCs and four CSUs.

The narratives of interdependence expressed thus far in this chapter by lower-SES students reflect a sense of concern and obligation regarding the needs of one's family when making a decision about the future. Such considerations were notably absent in the stories highlighted by their higher-SES peers, who, despite extensive familial support, viewed themselves as autonomous individuals who were making a decision that was in their own best interests. For lower-SES students, the concerns about pursuing higher education institutions beyond California also reflect worries about the emotional bonds they have developed with their families. Lower-SES students worried about the effects that separation from their families during their college years would have on their emotional well-being. This concern was present even when they were considering colleges within California, but it was much more pronounced when they thought about colleges beyond California. This is not a case of lower-SES students being overly worried; instead, it reflects how their family's social class positions (e.g., working class, low income) shape the experiences that they and their parents have (e.g., reliance on one another), which ultimately affects the considerations (e.g., emotional bonds, anticipated family obligations) that students draw on to think about which colleges are the right fit for them and their families.

Interdependence Grounded in Family Resistance

In addition to narratives of interdependence that emphasize family obligations and concern for the family's well-being, another aspect of this narrative focused on their family's overt resistance to them moving far from home for college. Some students not only anticipated family difficulties while in college but they also faced opposition from their parents against pursuing higher education far away from home. Jay, the son of Chinese immigrants, is a good example of this. Unlike other lower-SES students, Jay had many extended family members who graduated from college. Yet, despite his family being more familiar with the college process than other lower-SES families in the study, he still anticipated obstacles as to where he could attend college. This anticipation was grounded in his observation of the geographic constraints imposed on where his older cousins could attend college and his own struggle with his mother over the same issue. He recalled these constraints, alluding to the instance of a cousin trying to convince his parents to allow him to attend MIT:

> The family members want the children to go to the best schools, but also be relatively close. When he [the cousin] got accepted, he knew it was a good opportunity and he also got in to [UC] Berkeley. His mom didn't understand, "Why go all the way to Massachusetts when you can stay in the Bay and go there?" It's a great opportunity. They had this argument about whether he can go or not. His older brother had to intervene to explain to his mom. This is a wonderful opportunity for him. He's the one or one of the few from the family that went to college out of the UC system. His mom didn't really want him to go away. He comes home maybe twice or three times a year. She didn't want that. She wanted to see her son pretty often at least.

The failure of the parents in Jay's extended family to distinguish between various types of colleges played a role in their resistance to letting their children attend college across the country. Yet the larger issue was that parents were afraid of letting their children go through an experience alone that they themselves were unfamiliar with. Jay rationalized the resistance of parents: "They are not ready for you to grow up completely. They want to watch over you even though you are an adult." Students like Jay came to eventually internalize these worries as well, and it shaped how far from home they thought they could attend college. This was the case with Jay, who applied to four UCs, four CSUs, and an in-state private university. This narrative of interdependence, expressed in the anticipation of ongoing dependence between child and parents beyond high school, shaped his college choice decision making: "It's more convenient for the both of us. Say if I get homesick, being in [UC] Santa Cruz, it's only an hour and a half from Oakland if they want to see me or I want to see them or if there's a family emergency, it's a lot more convenient than if I went out of state or to SoCal [Southern California]."

It was more likely the case that students who faced family resistance toward pursuing higher education far from home were female students. Parents were especially concerned for the personal safety and well-being of their daughters. Maria, the child of Mexican immigrants, is one such student. While the struggles of her mother motivated Maria to obtain a higher education, Maria remained vigilant that family issues could be a potential obstacle:

MARIA: What if school gets hard? What if my family needs me? I can't just drop everything and leave. But honestly, I think I could do it. Cause my mom, she might need help and stuff, but she needs to understand that I am going to be away. There has to be another way for her to get help. My brother is going to be there too. I just have to be prepared to be worried and stuff but be prepared to keep moving forward. If I stay stuck on those worries and stress, it's not going to get me anywhere.

INTERVIEWER: Tell me more about the family thing. You say you might worry about your family.

MARIA: So what if my mom gets sick. She has hypertension so I worry about that all the time. My brother, he's 14. What if there's peer pressure and he becomes involved with something? What if my little siblings get injured? I always think about different situations. What if a family member passes away? I recently had that and that was really hard because I was finalizing my senior project and obviously I had to take time to go to the funeral and all that stuff. I just think about different situations and as much as I wish I could just come back and everything will be okay. Let's be realistic, I can't just drop everything and leave it. We have to move on. Just like how I have moved on from all of my other struggles. I just have to be prepared. That's what I think about.

Like her lower-SES peers, Maria was deeply concerned about her family's health and well-being. With their home in a neighborhood where gangs and drugs were prevalent, Maria was apprehensive about the vulnerability of her brother to such influences. Her mother's preexisting health condition added additional stress to her worries about the future. She tried her best to maintain a positive outlook and was adamant that she would continue on in her education even if such concerns materialized. In doing so, Maria was mentally preparing herself for the possibility of a future in which she may be unable to support her family in times of need.

Maria may have achieved some peace of mind with her outlook, but she also had to deal with pushback from her family about attending college away from home:

> My mom she was like, "You will go to Berkeley. You will get in." So she was like, "So you can be close and stuff." They know I'm her first kid going to college and I don't think she's ready to say bye. . . . She was like, "Berkeley's a good school," just because she's not ready to let me go alone to a new city, new place. She's like, "Don't walk to bad parts of LA because there's different parts of LA. I lived over there." It's complicated. . . . They were really encouraging me to stay.

Maria's narrative of interdependence, grounded in her recognition of her family's economic situation, her worries about the health and well-being of her family, and her mother's fears about letting her leave home for college, placed constraints on where she could attend college. Given the difficulties of justifying to her mother and herself about applying to UCLA, it was not surprising that Maria did not give any serious consideration to out-of-state colleges. Maria applied to only in-state universities: four UCs, four CSUs, and a couple of private colleges. In her reflections on all the factors that she took into account, being close to home was important: "Honestly, I thought about financial aid, and how close it is and I thought about, like, how academically well are they doing. That's what I thought about. . . . Being close to home is just, I guess, if I ever needed help or just even emotional help, my mom will be there. Just being close to my mom is really valuable for me."

Lily, the daughter of Vietnamese immigrants, was another student who faced pushback from her parents in pursuing higher education far from home. Lily strongly considered colleges on the East Coast, including Ivy League schools. But Lily's parents resisted that idea. Her parents pressed her to choose colleges close to home so that they could visit her and she could come back home whenever they needed her. As a result, distance from home became a key consideration in where she could apply to college. "My decision was also made based on how far away from them I will be. Number one they are getting older, I want to visit them as much as I can and to come back home when there's an emergency. And vice versa. Because they are afraid something might happen to me." Lily also had a health condition that worried her parents:

They say, "If you are across the country, how are we going to get to you when an emergency happens?" . . . One thing they always remind me of is my whole high blood pressure thing. . . . "Being two hours away, if something happens, we can come visit you at the hospital if you are there. But if you are eight hours away, what if no one drives us?" My dad is getting older, and his driving is weaker so he can't make the trip out there with my mom. That was the main point in my decision.

Lily deliberated with her parents and made the decision that she would apply only to California schools. She recalled, "Eventually, it was that I would only apply to schools within California but my compromise was that I would apply to schools in So-Cal [Southern California] and Nor-Cal [Northern California]." She applied to four UCs, four CSUs, and three in-state private colleges.

The resistance that Maria, Jay, and Lily face from their parents in where they should apply to college is distinctly different from the resistance higher-SES students face. The family aversions that higher-SES students encounter, if there are any at all, tend to center around the prestige of colleges. Higher-SES parents were likely to express concerns when their children entertained the prospect of applying to small liberal arts colleges that were not as well-known as private research universities. In contrast, lower-SES students faced family resistance primarily in regard to the geographic location of the institutions they considered. The emotional bonds between children and parents, the concern of parents about the safety and well-being of their children, and the recognition by parents that they are limited in their ability to reach their children if they are far from home for college contribute to the distinct family resistance that lower-SES students confront.

The narratives of interdependence among lower-SES students all highlight how the emotional and familial circumstances influence the considerations that students take into account when deciding where to submit college applications. Family narratives shape how being far away from home is framed as undesirable when it comes to choosing college. This understanding of distance from home is different from how their higher-SES peers utilize the same criteria in their selection of colleges. Due to their narratives of independence, higher-SES students actually framed being far from home for college as desirable and necessary for their personal growth.

Heterogeneity among Lower-SES Students

Although the majority of lower-SES students (eighteen of twenty-three) talked about their experiences and upbringings that reflected a narrative of interdependence like those already discussed in this chapter, there were exceptions to these patterns, and it is useful to highlight some of them as well. Some students, for example, did not express a narrative of interdependence because they did not anticipate their family to be a cause of concern or a source of obligation in the future. It was not the case that their families did not have any challenges. They did, but these students did not anticipate such challenges affecting them in the future. One student, Sarah, the daughter of Mexican immigrants, did not perceive any geographic restrictions because she was seeking to be far away from her family due to family conflicts: "There are a lot of family problems. I try to stay away from my stepfather because there are just family problems. I guess I don't want to be in that situation where there's argument and stuff and I try to avoid. So yeah because I'm not going to be near them, I don't feel like I should be near them."

Another student was Shen, the child of Vietnamese immigrants, who had to take care of his mother and younger brother, both of whom suffer from a degenerative eye disease. Despite the amount of responsibilities he had at home, he applied to colleges across the country. He anticipated relatives to step in and assist when he was away in college: "Although I have a lot of problems in my family, my mom and dad are very supportive of me going to a good college. They allow me to go anywhere in the United States. So I'm not limited to only California. And then I also have a few cousins that are willing to help my parents while I'm gone because they are around the community. If my mom or dad needs something, they will be there to help them."

The absence of a narrative of interdependence did not automatically mean that students would apply to out-of-state colleges. If students did not know much about out-of-state colleges or were unfamiliar with out-of-state environments, they were less likely to apply to such colleges. As an example, take the case of Anthony. Anthony, the son of an African American couple, did not express a narrative of interdependence. His parents actually encouraged him to go outside California for college. However, it was only after he had taken a trip to Hawaii through a program for low-income students and visited family members in Louisiana that he became comfortable at the prospect of living away from home. He ended up submitting college applications to out-of-state colleges.

Narratives of Independence among Higher-SES Students

Whereas socioeconomically disadvantaged students are raised in families in which they are more likely to develop a sense of constraint in their decision making, middle-class children grow up in families in which they are given opportunities and experiences to develop their sense of control and autonomy (Kohn and Schooler 1983; Lareau 2002; Calarco 2014). This greater sense of choice and autonomy among middle-class children is possible because middle-class families have the economic resources to accommodate the specific needs of their children. For instance, middle-class children lead highly structured lives centered on activities that are customized according to their needs and interests (Chin and Phillips 2004). Middle-class parents tend to stress the importance of self-direction by placing children in situations in which they must make and justify their decisions (Lareau and Weininger 2010). The result of these experiences is the development of a set of specific preferences and behaviors that shapes how students think about the social world and their decision making in different settings (Stuber 2009; Calarco 2014). The type of upbringing associated with middle-class families fosters a set of cultural dispositions that encourages students to seek out extracurricular activities and new experiences as a way to test their independence (Stuber 2009).

When discussing their decision-making processes, higher-SES students in this study presented narratives of independence regarding what they had done to prepare for college and where they applied. They emphasized aspects of their upbringing and experiences that demonstrated their initiative in identifying and deciding what activities they should participate in. They downplayed the influence of their parents in their decision making, and they saw themselves as individuals who are autonomous in choosing their directions and college options. Moreover, higher-SES students highlighted how family trips, summer camps, and other organized activities fostered their curiosity about places and things beyond their local environments. These aspects of the narratives of independence—initiative, curiosity, and autonomy—shaped how higher-SES students understood their past and how they thought about their future. As a result, higher-SES students framed college as an opportunity to leave their families and immerse themselves in an environment far from home.

The case of Scott, a multiracial student, exemplified the centrality of initiative and autonomy in higher SES-students' narratives of independence. His mother received a bachelor's degree, and his father briefly attended college before dropping out to start a business. Scott fondly remembered his father working with him in elementary school to help him overcome his speech impediment. While Scott acknowledged his parents' involvement in his life, he was quick to emphasize aspects that reflected his initiative and autonomy. This was readily seen in his discussion about the role of his parents in his life:

SCOTT: My dad never went to college so he doesn't involve himself too much. They are relatively hands off with me. I'm the only person who filled out the FAFSA [Free Application for Federal Student Aid] and college applications by myself. Since I was very young, they were like, "Fill out the paperwork and we'll sign the check for you. Just tell us what you are doing and why." I learned a lot of these things by myself.

INTERVIEWER: What did you think of that growing up, given that other kids have parents who are more hands on?

SCOTT: On the one hand, it was a bit intimidating. On the other hand, it was relatively liberating in that I understand how [to do] paperwork, you have

due dates, you have to manage your own deadlines, turn in stuff for
yourself. That's very . . . I hate to use the word, but it's very adult of me . . .
something I learned very early on. That was just expected in the real world.
No hand-holding. I have no complaints. I feel like I am better off for it. . . .
I think they're hands-off because they trust me. They set me up initially.
I wouldn't call them hands off in elementary but when I got to middle
school, I was a Boy Scout. This is the thing. For instance, I used to fly out to
San Diego to visit my grandparents. From an early age I packed my bag.
They just tell me what to do. It's like, "What do you want to do for the
summer?" I'm like, "I want to do this and this over the summer." "So circle
them on the booklet and tell me what weeks you want to do what." It's like I
knew, I chose what I did by myself and I organized it. They just provided
help, finding me a ride or something.

Scott projected a narrative of independence that relied on identifying
moments that demonstrated his initiative and autonomy. Though Scott
depended on his parents in that they paid for his activities, he was more focused
on how he was able to identify and choose his activities. He minimized the
involvement of his parents and stressed the centrality of his own efforts in
organizing his experiences. He viewed his parents' relatively low involvement
in his life as a sign of his maturity. This was different from how lower-SES students spoke of their experiences. Lower-SES students viewed the lack of parental involvement as a constraint in that they were unable to depend on their
parents for guidance, while some higher-SES students like Scott framed it as
an instance of their initiative and autonomy.

This narrative of independence shaped how Scott understood and approached
higher education. Scott relished the opportunity to attend college outside California. Being far away from home was a key criterion in his college search
because he wanted to extend his independence from his parents. He stated,
"I just want my parents to not be able to say, 'Why don't you come home for the
weekend?' That was my only requirement for distance. I expected to be out of
state." Scott was unconcerned about having to return home for the holidays or
during school breaks, a reflection of his social class upbringing in which his parents have provided financial support for his activities and experiences. Scott ended
up applying to one CSU, multiple UCs, an in-state private university, and multiple
out-of-state public and private universities on the West Coast and the East Coast.

Anna, who is the daughter of European immigrants who both completed
postgraduate degrees, emphasized how her parents fostered her curiosity and
sense of independence by encouraging her to explore her interests:

I don't think they ever forced me to do anything. I'm lucky. I got to figure that
out for myself. I think they got this from Europe or something. They are like,

"You will get to do what you want to do when you get to college. You can do anything and it's completely fine. You don't have to figure it out until you are 21." Because of that I have the freedom to figure out for myself what is it that I want to do. It's helpful because I would stick to this and be more motivated to do it because it's my idea and not someone else's idea.

While her parents encouraged her to explore different interests, Anna was adamant that it was not them but she who initiated these activities, a common theme in the narrative of independence among higher-SES students. Anna's narrative of independence was bolstered by her experiences traveling abroad. Through her parents' social connections and financial support, Anna was able to explore several countries in Europe. While some visits had been with her parents, she made the recent trips by herself; for example, she traveled to Switzerland during the summer before her senior year. These trips cultivated her curiosity about experiences and places different from where she grew up, which influenced her interest in colleges outside California: "I didn't think about it as I'm going away from home. It's like I'm just going someplace different. . . . I have absolutely no problem going to school there [far away]. I want to go on adventures. I want to experience the world. That means I have to leave California. I love traveling to new places so I'll be fine."

Instead of viewing her attendance at a college beyond California as being away from her family, Anna framed it as an opportunity to be exposed to a new set of experiences. This understanding of higher education was made possible by the experiences she was able to accumulate because of her parents' social class background and by her perceived autonomy in making decisions about her future. Anna applied to over twenty-plus colleges, including in-state colleges like the UCs and private colleges; out-of-state colleges, such as Ivy Leagues and liberal arts colleges; and colleges abroad in England.

While most higher-SES students portrayed their parents as hands-off or only moderately involved, several students described their parents as being heavily involved in their lives. These were typically Asian American students. Lan was one such student who talked about his parents as being active in shaping his direction throughout his life. Lan's parents decided to move the family to the United States from China so that he could take advantage of the U.S. educational system. Yet, despite the greater involvement on the part of his parents, the consequence was not a perceived sense of constraint but rather a developed sense of curiosity and autonomy in his decision making. For instance, Lan occasionally accompanied his father, who worked for an environmental nonprofit, across the country and even abroad when his father gave lectures on university campuses: "I think they've [my parents] always tried to expose me to different things, especially my dad. He takes me on his trips to see different parts, see different things. I get to see his environmental work in Tibet. So you know he's showing me that I can do whatever I like to do. That's also good for college. I think generally they are pretty open. They didn't force me to do anything that I didn't really want to."

Lan made it clear that he did not feel coerced by his parents to go on these trips. Instead, he viewed the trips as opportunities to be exposed to new things and places. In doing so, he kept his autonomy intact. This developed sense of curiosity motivated him to become involved with an organization at his high school that took students around the world to build schools in developing countries. With this organization, Lan traveled to Nepal and Haiti. These experiences shaped his desire to move out of his local environment for college: "I think just expanding my horizon. Maturing as a person. Learning practical skills. I feel like I am pretty mature, I think, for myself, but I don't have any practical skills that I can apply in a job situation. Getting some of that, expanding, getting to know the world better. I just think it brings a lot of different opportunities. If I don't go, I would be stuck [in the Bay]. Not much going on in here."

Lan framed college as an opportunity to move beyond his comfort zone and to experience as much of the world as possible. This framing was made possible by his trips across the country and around the world, which have instilled in him a sense of curiosity of faraway places and a sense of autonomy about choosing his path. Lan specifically targeted many colleges outside California that would enable him to satisfy these expectations. When asked about some of the characteristics he looked for in a college, he replied, "I knew that I wanted to go somewhere on the East Coast so I looked at mostly East Coast schools." Lan applied to five UCs, six Ivy Leagues, three out-of-state and one in-state liberal arts college, and another private out-of-state university.

Although students like Lan, Anna, and Scott all had supportive parents that gave them space to explore their own interests, not all higher-SES students had such good relationships with their parents. However, this did not necessarily inhibit their sense of autonomy. Emily, for example, the daughter of two Chinese American professionals, described her family upbringing as one that was conflict-ridden. She and her parents have clashed over her grades, her involvement in extracurricular activities, and her potential college majors. Despite these issues with her parents, she did not anticipate her family to be a hindrance: "I would say that they [my parents] were never really an obstacle. What they say is somewhat discouraging but I don't think I listen to my parents as much as other kids listen to their parents. My parents and I are separated by language barriers. Communication has always been really tough. Sometimes we say you think that way and I think this way. It's different cultures, generations. We've never really connected. It's okay if you feel this way because I feel this [other] way."

Emily reduced the conflict between herself and her parents to a matter of cultural misunderstanding. In doing so, she did not perceive her family to be an issue that shaped how she made her decisions. Despite the heavy involvement of her parents in the college application process, as evidenced by their hiring a private college counselor for her, she was dismissive of their contributions to her situation: "They didn't really prepare me. It was me getting myself through to college. Everything else, once again, I can't explain. I just thought it was known that to get into a good college, I needed to succeed in high school."

By minimizing the influence of her parents in her own decision making, Emily was able to project a sense of autonomy. This narrative of independence is bolstered by her middle-class background, which provided her with multiple opportunities to travel beyond California and outside the country with a chorus group based out of San Francisco. She traveled to New York and Italy to perform with this group. These experiences and her upbringing cultivated a desire to be away from her family for college. Emily applied to in-state as well as out-of-state colleges that included the UCs, Ivy League universities, several liberal arts colleges in the Midwest, and other private research universities across the country.

Conclusion

Students' decisions about which colleges to apply to were not merely a straightforward consideration of the costs and benefits of various college options. Instead these decisions were intimately linked to students' social class backgrounds. In other words, students' decisions were informed not only by their knowledge of different types of college institutions but also by their understanding of the type of social experiences they had accumulated and the type that they wanted to pursue while in college. Choosing where to go to college was as much about the institutional qualities of colleges as it was about the particular type of lifestyle that students desired, a reflection of their social class experiences and upbringings.

The upbringings and experiences associated with students' social class backgrounds shaped their narratives regarding how much autonomy or constraints they perceived in making college decisions. Higher-SES students presented a narrative of independence about what they had done to prepare themselves for college and where they applied. In contrast, lower-SES students spoke of experiences and considerations that reflected a narrative of interdependence between themselves and their parents that was grounded in the mutual concern they had for one another as the prospect of college loomed. As a result, higher-SES students framed college as an opportunity to leave their families and immerse themselves in an environment far from home while lower-SES students understood college as a continuation of family interdependence. Consequently, higher-SES students applied to selective private and public universities in California and other parts of the country, while most lower-SES students limited their choices to colleges closer to home in California.

In the narratives offered by students from each social class, both highlighted certain aspects of students' upbringing and experiences. These narratives reflected students' understandings of their social and economic circumstances; they were students' interpretations about their upbringing and experiences. While lower-SES students projected a narrative of interdependence, it could be argued that lower-SES students, given what they had to overcome to become high-achieving students, were just as prepared to be independent as higher-SES students. However, the immediate and anticipated family responsibilities that lower-SES students faced, while preparing them for adulthood, also put an immense weight on their shoulders when they were making decisions about their future. Lower-SES students frequently spoke about their anxieties regarding their family's well-being and how their absence during college could exacerbate family issues. In the stories they told, lower-SES students rarely focused on their resilience or independence and instead spoke more about interdependence and family obstacles. For instance, rather than view the lack of involvement of their parents in the college application process as a sign of their independence or autonomy, many lower-SES students interpreted it as a drawback when they compared themselves to middle class-children who were more likely to receive parental support.

Conversely, even though higher-SES students chose to highlight themes of independence and initiative, their lives could also be construed as dependence on their parents. Indeed, studies of middle- and upper-middle-class families consistently show that parents are heavily involved in the lives of their children; as a result, children relied on their parents' social, cultural, and economic capital to help them procure advantages in educational settings and beyond (Lareau 2002; Lareau and Weininger 2010; Calarco 2014; Hamilton 2016). While dependence can be a valid argument, it is a claim based on the behaviors of students and not how students interpreted their experiences. How students understand their experiences can be different from how others perceive them (Weiss, Cipollone, and Jenkins 2014). In this study, higher-SES students interpreted their upbringing and experiences as demonstrating their autonomy, and they projected this understanding to their college choice decision making. While they mentioned their parents' financial and academic support throughout their lives, this was overshadowed by their emphasis on their own initiative and independence in making their decisions.

Another key distinction between the two narratives was how they were constructed. In the narratives of interdependence, lower-SES students projected onto their future what they had experienced and observed—present-day challenges were still expected to be ongoing problems. In contrast, in the narratives of independence, higher-SES students were aware that because of their social class advantages, they were perceived by others as being more dependent on their parents for their academic success. Thus many higher-SES students made a concerted effort to portray their experiences as demonstrating their own autonomy and initiative rather than reliance on their parents.

To minimize the influence of their parents, higher-SES students drew on two strategies. One was to downplay the involvement of their parents. Most higher-SES students spoke about the involvement of their parents in their lives, but the influences of their parents were relegated to the margins. Students acknowledged that they had parents who provided them with the resources to make their goals a reality, but their aspirations were theirs alone. Their parents were depicted as giving them the freedom to develop and pursue their own interests. The other approach higher-SES students took was to compare their own experience to that of another classmate or to a generalized other whose parents were much more involved and restrictive. The respondent's autonomy in this case was then highlighted as a contrast to the constraints of the other student. This need for higher-SES students to emphasize their independence and autonomy was not surprising because students were well aware that they had to stand out among the competitive college applicant crowd. One way to do this was to provide a counternarrative to the perception that they were privileged or dependent individuals.

Though social class structured the narratives that students expressed, the elements that students brought up in their narratives were shaped by differences in social background, such as race, gender, and immigrant background. For instance, among lower-SES students, females were more likely to emphasize parental resistance, children of immigrants felt more of an obligation to support their family, and Asian American students were much more concerned about the challenges that their parents, who were limited in their ability to speak English, would face in their absence. Hispanic students, unlike their Asian American and African American peers, did not seriously consider any colleges beyond California. Part of the reason was a lack of exposure through schools and college preparation programs. Another could be the immigration status of their parents. Two Hispanic students spoke specifically about parents who lacked legal immigrant documentation.

Among higher-SES students, Asian American students faced greater pressure from their parents to submit applications to the nation's elite private universities, specifically Ivy League universities. Asian American students who applied to less prominent universities like small liberal arts colleges faced skepticism from their parents about their college choices. However, the fact that these students also submitted applications to Ivy League universities helped to quell the concerns of their parents. The constraints Asian American students faced from their parents did not place spatial restrictions on their consideration of colleges.

Ultimately, this chapter contributes to a better understanding of the mechanisms by which social inequality is reproduced across generations. The concept of narratives captured how this process unfolded over time through a multitude of experiences. Through narratives, this chapter demonstrated that the importance of family considerations in where students apply to college cannot be reduced merely to a value devoid of any concrete experiences. Rather, the decision about whether to apply to colleges across the country was based on experiences and observations that students had accumulated over the years. Class-based socialization practices played a central role. Childrearing among most higher-SES families combined with students' repeated exposure to new experiences and environments over time cultivated their children's confidence about their ability to thrive far from home. These multiple experiences led to the development of a sense of autonomy and curiosity that emboldened higher-SES students to seek colleges outside California. Among lower-SES students, exposure to a life of economic deprivation, family responsibilities, and family health concerns placed spatial constraints on their consideration of colleges.

Conclusion

● ●

Despite the numerous obstacles the lower-SES students interviewed for this book encountered on their journey to college, they had all managed to reach levels of academic achievement relatively similar to those of their more advantaged peers. High academic achievement, however, did not mean that lower-SES students were in the same position as their higher-SES peers to take full advantage of the college opportunities that were available to them upon graduation. Indeed, as discussed throughout this book, lower SES-students made calculations in their college decision making that were very different from those of higher SES-students. Although lower-SES students did apply to many colleges in California that higher SES-students also applied to, they decided against applying to many other top schools that higher-SES students applied to, particularly schools that were far from where they grew up and far from their parents and family, or schools where they believed they might not fit in. In the end, of the students interviewed for this book, the overwhelming majority of higher-SES students (twenty-one of twenty-three) submitted applications to out-of-state colleges, and many applied to small liberal arts colleges and Ivy League universities. In contrast, most lower-SES students (sixteen of twenty-three) confined their choices of colleges to those close to home in California, applying primarily to in-state public universities. The decisions lower-SES students made about where to apply to college—and which could have immense ramifications for their social and economic mobility—can only partly be explained by their academic records. To truly understand the college decision-making process of both lower- and higher-SES students, it is necessary to look beyond academic achievement and to consider their knowledge and experiences rooted in their schools, families, and communities. In doing so, it is possible to see how, for all students, choosing where to go to college was as much about the particular type of lifestyle that students wanted to pursue during college as it was about the institutional qualities of colleges. Lifestyle preferences that informed students' choices of college largely reflected their social class experiences and upbringing.

The stories of the students discussed in this book make clear how social class background is intricately linked to college choices. As students moved through the different stages of the college choice decision-making process, key aspects of their social class influenced their thinking, giving rise to the narratives and framing strategies they used to understand college in their lives. By linking students' choices to their social class positions and their specific individual experiences, this book elucidates the constraints that social environments impose on students, while also highlighting the agency of individuals as they navigate the decision-making process. It points to the extraordinary scope of influence that social class has on the college choice decision-making process—from committing to college attendance to preparing for college and finally to submitting college applications. Social class experiences, knowledge, and understandings rooted in the family, school, academic programs, and community shaped what students thought about their future, their postsecondary educational options, and ultimately where they applied to college. In doing so, this book also brings into view how students' structural positions (their social class backgrounds) and cultural contexts (social class–based experiences and understandings) need to be considered together to understand seemingly individual decisions about where students submitted college applications.

How Social Class Matters

To help demonstrate the impact of social class background on college choices, this book used several specific concepts drawn from the culture and cognition framework—frames, schemas, and narratives. Each of these concepts draws our attention to the different ways that social class background and experiences influence how students make sense of their lives and their postsecondary educational options. Most lower-SES students grew up under very different circumstances than their higher-SES peers. These conceptual lenses help provide a view on how the information, experiences, and understandings that students draw on to make their decisions largely reflect the different social class circumstances of their lives.

As discussed in detail in chapters 1 and 2, students framed the idea of college in their lives in different ways according to their social class. Students' framings of these two stages in the college choice process shaped the nature of their decision making and their behaviors. For example, higher-SES students framed college attendance as inevitable and a natural progression of schooling. As a result, they took for granted college attendance and assumed from a very young age that college was the next and only appropriate path after high school. Given their assumption about the inevitability of college attendance, higher-SES students framed college preparation as a matter of doing what was necessary to stand out among their peers and other competitive applicants for admissions into top colleges. Higher-SES students knew they were going to college; it was just a matter of where they would attend and how to position themselves for the top colleges.

The social environment of higher-SES students gave rise to their specific frame regarding college attendance and college preparation. Growing up in a social environment in which almost everyone went to college, higher-SES students did not think twice about whether they themselves should go to college. College represented the natural next step for them after high school. Similarly, higher-SES students did not question their preparedness for college; they were confident that they would succeed in college because others around them had successfully completed college. Given this understanding, higher-SES students' focus on college preparation was primarily about distinguishing themselves from other similarly qualified students.

On the other hand, most lower-SES students framed college as one of multiple options after high school. The completion of high school represented a key transitional point that required deliberation about what to do next. These students needed to accumulate knowledge and experiences to convince themselves that college was the right path for them. For most lower-SES students, many of whom are the first in their family to pursue a higher education, the decision to attend college was one that was consciously pursued. Lower-SES students had to actively work toward going to college. Even then, college still occupied a tentative prospect in their future. Despite being highly qualified, lower-SES students were worried about their chances of being admitted and their success in college. Lower-SES students expressed these concerns in the doubts and hesitancy they had regarding college attendance and in their disappointment at their high schools' quality of instruction, curriculum, and college-related resources.

As a result, lower-SES students framed college preparation as making sure they were prepared for the challenges of a new and unfamiliar academic environment as well as demonstrating to colleges that they were well-rounded students. College preparation involved lower-SES students seeking resources outside their high schools to develop the skills and habits necessary to succeed at the next level. Rather than emphasize their distinctiveness from others (as higher-SES students did), most lower-SES students centered their college-preparation strategy around demonstrating that they were academically competent and socially involved.

In addition to students' framing strategies, there were other key factors that played a role in influencing their decision-making process, specifically the narratives they used to define themselves as discussed in chapter 4, and the kinds of colleges that high schools and college preparation programs presented to students as appropriate options for postgraduation—the college schemas discussed in chapter 3. Although all students acted independently in notable ways, they also clearly drew from these schemas to make sense of where they should consider submitting college applications. These schemas took on significant clout for students, and high schools and college preparation programs regularly reinforced the hierarchy of choices they depicted. In the case of the high schools in particular, these college schemas were reflected in the suggestions of teachers and counselors, the application behaviors of alumni, and the colleges that came to the high schools to recruit students, all of which augmented the schemas' clout among students.

For higher-SES students, their high schools offered a *selective college anywhere* schema in which they were socialized to believe that top colleges across the country were viable options for them. Higher-SES students were well aware of this schema when they talked about the colleges that visited their high school, the college suggestions that they received from their school's college matching software program, and the college destinations of alumni. In a way, higher-SES students endeavored to replicate the success of past students by trying to gain admissions into those colleges or similar ones. On the other hand, lower-SES students—who were mostly offered an *in-state four-year college* schema that encouraged them to submit applications to primarily four-year public universities—most lower-SES students submitted applications to the colleges and universities in both the UC and CSU systems and to some in-state private colleges. Only a third of the lower-SES student sample submitted applications to out-of-state colleges, even though more students encountered the *selective college anywhere* schema from their programs or high schools, demonstrating that exposing high-achieving, lower-SES students to top schools is not by itself enough to mitigate the significant divergence between lower and higher SES college applications patterns.

As discussed in chapter 3, these schemas that high schools and college preparation programs present to students make some choices more likely than others, but they don't necessarily guarantee a specific set of decisions from a group of students. This is because the influence of schemas is mediated by students' experiences, personal preferences, and understandings that they bring to the decision-making process.

Drawing on their understandings and experiences, students presented narratives that helped them define themselves. These narratives influenced how they made their decision about where to submit college applications. One of the key sources of this kind of narrative for students was their families. Family upbringing and experiences shaped students' choices of college. Among lower-SES students, exposure to a life of economic deprivation, family responsibilities, and family health concerns forced students to think about the ongoing role they play in the health and success of their families. Consequently, they understood college as a continuation of family interdependence, leading them to select colleges close to home that would enable them to be available to assist in case of family emergencies.

On the other hand, in the case of higher-SES students, students' repeated exposure to new experiences and new environments away from home led to the development of a sense of curiosity and autonomy. When combined with the absence of an expectation or obligation to support their family during college, higher-SES students framed college as an opportunity for independence and self-exploration away from the familiar routines of their home environment.

The importance of family considerations in where students apply to college cannot be reduced merely to a value devoid of any concrete experiences. It was not that lower-SES students did not have any interest in applying to top colleges beyond California. They did. But their family experiences and observations imposed constraints on where they could realistically attend college. The opposite was true for higher-SES students, many of whom developed an interest in attending college far from home because of the positive experiences and observations that they had accumulated over the years about living away from home. Both groups of students valued top colleges, but only higher-SES students had the experiences and resources needed for them to make sense of top colleges outside California as viable and personally desirable options.

Social Reproduction of Inequality

Academic success alone does not guarantee that lower-SES students will end up in social and economic positions similar to those of their higher-SES peers. Because the experiences and understandings that lower-SES students accumulate outside schools are just as important as how well they perform in the classroom, and because these experiences and understandings outside the classroom directly affect their ability to attend—or even imagine attending—top colleges, social inequality will continue to persist, even among students of similar ability or qualifications. The social class gap in knowledge, resources, and experiences between lower-SES and higher-SES students contributes to unequal opportunities and different outlooks that put students on different mobility trajectories. Most lower-SES students in this study are destined for large public universities, whereas their higher-SES peers are set on smaller, private research universities and small liberal arts colleges. This has implications for the type of educational experience that students will receive and their mobility prospects once they complete college.

These diverging attendance trends are directly influenced by the types of opportunities and experiences students received prior to college. Throughout high school, higher-SES students had access to a wide array of opportunities and experiences that shaped their ability to imagine attending top schools, even when they are far from home: some participated in musical or athletic groups that performed or competed across the state, the country, and even abroad. Others worked with renowned university faculty on research projects that are typically available only to graduate students and postdoctoral fellows. Many participated in academic camps or special interest summer camps across the country. Some traveled abroad to complete community service projects. Due to these experiences, higher-SES students had an understanding of college as an opportunity for exploration, self-discovery, and career exposure. These social class advantages will enable higher-SES students to seek out and take advantage of different enrichment activities that college has to offer, such as study abroad programs, summer internships, or faculty-sponsored research. In doing so, higher-SES students will likely develop the knowledge, experiences, and social connections during college that are highly valued when they seek employment and postgraduate opportunities. The opportunities for higher-SES students during high school were available to them because of the social connections of their parents, their parents' financial support, and the resources of their high schools and communities. Sadly, it seemed as if high academic achievement was the only thing that most lower-SES students had in common with their higher-SES peers.

While most higher-SES students were motivated by the need to distinguish themselves from others through activities and different types of nonacademic experiences, lower-SES students primarily focused on college readiness—understanding what college is like and developing the skills and habits to succeed in college. It is clearly important for lower-SES students to devote attention to college readiness (many were the first in their family to go to college, and learning what to expect and preparing for college standards was essential for their success in college). Yet, when compared to the experiences of higher-SES students, it is also abundantly clear that the emphasis on college preparation left out the cultivation of other skills or outlooks that could benefit lower-SES students beyond just the classroom, including in ways that could help them develop the dispositions and opportunities necessary to reach their full potential.

The Influence of Race, Gender, and Immigrant Background on College Choices

Although shining a light on the influence of social class on students' decisions about where to attend college is the primary objective of this book, social class is not the only important factor influencing the educational experiences, outlooks, and decisions of students. Among lower-SES students, Asian American students tended to benefit from resources that were not typically available to students of other racial and ethnic backgrounds. For instance, Asian American students in the study were more likely to have older siblings or immediate relatives who had gone to a four-year college. While all of the lower-SES students in this study are first-generation college students, the fact that some Asian American students had personal connections to someone who had attended college helped them better navigate the college decision-making process.

Asian American children also benefited from the availability of ethnic resources that promote educational achievement and college attendance. For instance, Asian parents, especially Chinese parents, heard about educational opportunities, programs, and colleges from their personal social networks or via the ethnic media. Some parents put their children in such programs to receive additional assistance on the path toward college attendance. Many Asian parents talked to their children about attending the top colleges in California and sometimes across the country, even though they expressed hesitation and reluctance at the thought of their children being far away from home for college.

Additionally, Asian American students were more likely to attend high schools that were relatively better quality than those of their Hispanic and African American peers. While Hispanic and African American students attended schools in their district that were considered among the lowest performing, Asian American students typically went to schools that were in the middle range, were more socioeconomically diverse, or had special academic programs. Moreover, among college preparation programs, Asian American students were more likely to participate in the programs that specifically recruited high-achieving students with the aim of exposing them to top private colleges across the country. Meanwhile, Hispanic and African American students were more likely to enroll in general college preparation programs that sought to put students in colleges, especially public four-year colleges. While some of these racial differences in access to the type of high schools and college preparation programs did not result in more Asian American students applying to out-of-state colleges, they still had an impact on students' level of preparation and their approach toward applying to colleges within California.

The role of gender was most visible when it came to students' choices of colleges. While the parents of most lower-SES students preferred that their children stay close to home for college, female students faced the most resistance when they entertained thoughts of going far away to college, even if it was within California. For instance, one Asian American female student had to compromise with her parents just to apply to colleges throughout California. She initially considered out-of-state colleges, but her parents pressed her to stay close to home. The resolution was that her parents allowed her to apply to colleges in Northern California, where she lived, as well as in Southern California. A Hispanic female student was also discouraged from Southern California colleges and universities as well because her parents felt it was dangerous for her to be attending a school in the region. She still applied to colleges in that region, but it took a lot of self-reassurances to make that decision.

The obstacles young women faced were not limited just to familial resistance to their going far away to college. Female students were typically more involved at home, tending to household duties or looking after their younger siblings. As such, it was not merely external barriers that they encountered in the college choice process. They also had to navigate feelings of guilt about leaving behind those responsibilities as they pursued higher education.

Similarly, those students that were children of immigrants and from lower-SES families consistently felt obligated to continue to look after the welfare of their parents and siblings. These individuals recognized the sacrifices their parents had made and continued to make. As a consequence, deciding where to attend college was not merely about students following what was in their individual best interests but also taking into account the needs of their family. Asian American children were more likely to have older parents who did not speak English fluently. Thus Asian American students had to intervene on their parents' behalf when their parents needed assistance engaging with outside institutions. These kinds of obligations directly constrained students' consideration of what college they could attend.

Hispanic students had less of the direct responsibilities because it seemed that their parents were relatively better able to navigate outside the home on their own. However, Hispanic students faced an additional barrier that Asian American students did not encounter. A couple of Hispanic students indirectly referenced the immigration status and documentation issues of their parents. One student specifically talked about how this made it difficult for him to consider colleges outside California because it would be very difficult for his parents to get to him.

Despite the constraints that family obligations had on lower-SES Asian American students from immigrant families, higher-SES Asian American students whose parents were immigrants did not highlight family obligations as a specific constraint in their college selection process. Instead, much like the rest of their higher-SES peers, these Asian American students understood their future to be really about themselves as individuals—making decisions to enhance their own experiences and opportunities.

Among higher-SES students, however, there were still important differences in their college decision making based on race. For example, among higher-SES students, it was clear that parents of Asian American students were much more likely to be heavily involved in their children's educational trajectory. Asian American parents communicated to their children the particular colleges they should consider. When students considered lesser known colleges, especially liberal arts colleges, parents were often against the idea of their attending those schools. However, the fact that students also applied to brand name colleges like the top UCs and Ivy League universities helped to quell some of the parents' concerns. Some Asian parents were much more hands on than others, dictating what students should or should not do outside their classes and academics. Others were personally involved in the college preparation process or paid for professional assistance in test preparation or essay composition.

Policy Implications

Given the low numbers of lower-SES students that apply to and attend the nation's top colleges, it is essential that new interventions be undertaken to ensure that lower-SES, high-achieving students are able to take full advantage of higher education opportunities. This book's findings point to two categories of interventions that could make an important difference. These interventions, outlined in this final section of the book, are not mutually exclusive, and it may even be necessary to combine the two approaches to effectively ensure that high-achieving, lower-SES students are able to take full advantage of the opportunities available to them and fulfill their highest potential. Given their high ability, it is imperative that lower-SES students be put in the best position possible to pursue the nation's top colleges and universities and to fully reap the benefits of a college education.

One area where intervention is needed and could play a significant role in addressing the unequal access among students to top colleges is to address the social class gap in knowledge, experiences, and opportunities that separate lower-SES students from their higher-SES peers during high school. This would entail making sure that lower-SES students are able to participate in opportunities and experiences that are typically not available to them due to the absence of social and financial capital. For instance, in the realm of internships, programs may need to specifically recruit students from disadvantaged backgrounds. Rather than post opportunities and wait for whomever applies, programs need to conduct targeted outreach to groups who are less likely to know about such opportunities. Merely publicizing something will do little to decrease inequality in access; instead, individuals with more social and financial resources are the ones most likely to benefit.

Closing the information gap between higher-SES and lower-SES students would also play an essential role in this broader intervention. Lower-SES students are less likely to have access to accurate information about the different quality of colleges and about the financial cost and financial aid of these top colleges (Plank and Jordan 2001; Kelly and Schneider 2011; Radford 2013; Smith, Pender, and Howell 2013). In other words, lower-SES students need to be informed about the different types of colleges available across the United States, not just in their region, and about the consequences of attending different types of colleges. For instance, how is the experience at a large public university different from that of a small liberal arts college versus that of an Ivy League university? Many lower-SES students know about public universities in California, but few know about small liberal arts colleges. These students have heard about Ivy League universities, but many are discouraged by the sticker prices of these institutions. Many top private colleges have already eliminated costs related to tuition, room, and board for students from low-income and working-class families (Hoxby and Avery 2012). Targeted outreach that informs lower-SES students about the availability of aid for students like them would be a more effective approach than a generic pamphlet that is marketed toward students of all backgrounds.

Information by itself will likely not be sufficient to convince a significant number of lower-SES students to shift their college application choices. Concerns about fitting in at these institutions and about being far away from home will continue to exist. As such, providing exposure to experiences in other parts of the country and mentorship from current students at these institutions are additional measures that can be implemented. These kinds of strategies—which would involve socialization via the accumulation of positive experiences and personal connections—can help students cultivate a desire to attend one of the nation's top colleges. For example, among the lower-SES students who submitted applications to out-of-state colleges, there was one notable common denominator in their profiles: they had accumulated experiences that made them classify those colleges not just as appropriate but also desirable. Some of these experiences involved living in new parts of the country away from family for an extended period of time as part of an academic program or some nonacademic exploration program. These experiences helped alleviate some of their fears about living in new and different social and physical environments.

Similarly, to address lower-SES students' concerns about fitting in at these institutions, mentorship programs that connect these lower-SES students with current students from similar backgrounds may help. Higher-SES students already have such social connections via their family, friends, or alumni of their high schools. In the absence of such connections, lower-SES students must find other ways to make these personal connections. One way is through mentorship programs that pair them with current students. To be able to learn about an institution from someone they know and trust will make it that much more personal and convincing. These programs can take place during high school students' junior year, or even earlier, as they begin to ponder their college choices.

The second broader intervention would be to shift the narratives and frames that lower-SES students draw on to make their decisions. The cultural understandings that inform lower-SES students' narratives and frames shape how students think about higher education and viable college choices. These cultural understandings are typically the direct result of the experiences that students have accumulated. Although any intervention that will help close the social class gap in experiences will also play an important role in helping successfully modify how lower-SES students approach the college choice decision-making process, experiences by themselves may not necessarily translate into cultural understandings that make top colleges and universities desirable options. As a result, efforts must also be devoted toward helping students intentionally craft narratives about themselves and frames about higher education that will make them receptive to the idea of attending top colleges and universities that may be far from home.

For instance, in the case of narratives, efforts could be made to help lower-SES students intentionally focus on their resilience in overcoming countless obstacles to become high-achieving students. Instead of merely a narrative of interdependence, it is possible for students to craft multiple alternative narratives that make pursuing colleges far from home personally desirable. A narrative that shifts from that of family interdependence to include that of resilience, adaptation, and independence will help lower-SES students focus on their strengths to succeed whatever the conditions may be, instead of just the struggles and worries that have accompanied their lives.

Relatedly, shifting how lower-SES students frame higher education can also help with making top colleges and universities, regardless of location, far more appealing to students facing familial and financial constraints. If students frame college as merely just additional education after high school, it is harder to distinguish between different types of colleges and universities. Instead, if college is viewed as an opportunity for exploration and personal growth, it becomes much easier to identify how some colleges provide superior resources and experiences to help students enhance their understanding of themselves, their social surroundings, and what career they will pursue. Since top colleges and universities typically have many more resources and opportunities to offer than their less selective peers, this frame could help make these institutions more appealing to lower-SES students facing other constraints. Additionally, such a frame will prepare students to seek out these extracurricular activities, research, and internship opportunities once they are in college, encouraging lower-SES students to take full advantage of all that is available to them, instead of missing out on potential opportunities and experiences.

Acknowledgments

This book would not have been possible without the participation, support, or encouragement of many people. The research for this book was conducted as part of my dissertation project in the Department of Sociology at the University of California, Berkeley. I am indebted to the high school teachers, college preparation program staff, and other individuals who helped recruit their students for this research. I thank the students for their willingness to share their life stories with me.

While writing the dissertation, I benefited from constructive feedback from my dissertation chair David Harding and committee members Cybelle Fox, Susan Holloway, and Tom Gold. The Graduate Fellows Program, based out of the Institute for the Study of Societal Issues at UC Berkeley, played an invaluable role in helping me craft my initial arguments and complete the first two chapters. My participation in the program provided me with a sense of belonging that had eluded me as both a Hmong American and a first-generation college student during most of my graduate school career. I am immensely grateful to Deborah Lustig, David Minkus, and Christine Trost of the Graduate Fellows Program for their understanding of the challenges that confront students from underrepresented backgrounds and for their willingness to do what it takes to make sure that students like me finish our degrees and succeed after graduation.

I am grateful for my meeting with Lisa Banning, an editor at Rutgers University Press, who saw the potential for a book based on my research. I thank Lisa for what she did; it may seem like a small gesture, perhaps something that she did regularly as part of her job responsibilities, but to me, that meeting provided me with the affirmation and validation that I needed to move forward with my book manuscript.

In the process of working on my book proposal and finalizing my book manuscript, I benefited from the support of several colleagues in the Department of Sociology at the University of California, Merced. I cannot thank Laura Hamilton enough for the constructive feedback and encouragement she provided me at critical junctures of this process. There were many times where I felt stuck, and a meeting with Laura provided me with a sense of direction and the spark necessary to continue moving forward with the project. I thank Tanya Golash-Boza for providing valuable feedback on an earlier draft of my book proposal and Irenee Beattie for the close reading of one of the chapters. Charlie Eaton also provided important information about the book production process that helped to alleviate some of my worries. Amanda Mireles provided much needed motivation and encouragement throughout the process as well. Ma Vang from Critical Race and Ethnic Studies gave valuable advice about navigating the book manuscript process as well.

The structure and content of this book have benefited immensely from the editing done by Yia Lee and Christopher Lura. Yia read two chapters and Christopher read the whole manuscript. They both provided valuable suggestions that have strengthened the overall writing and readability of the book. I also want to thank the production team at Rutgers University Press, especially Peggy Solic and Kim Guinta, for their efforts in turning the manuscript into an actual book.

This books represents the culmination of an educational journey that began when I was an undergraduate. My trajectory to this point would not have been possible without the personal and academic support that I received as an undergraduate at Stanford University from many peers (Eric Shih, Hai Binh Nguyen, Timmy Lu, Linda Lee, and Linda Tran), staff (Cindy Ng and Shelley Tadaki), and professors (Carolyn Wong and Rachel Joo). They fostered my interests in issues of inequalities and cultivated my desire to conduct research.

Finally, I want to express my gratitude to my family members and friends. I thank my parents Leng Lor and Song Thao for their support of all my educational endeavors. As Hmong refugees from Laos who never attended school, my parents supported me in any way they could. I couldn't have completed this book without my wife (Anna) and kids (Julian and Sophie), who gave me the motivation and the space to work through my ideas and writing in peace. My siblings, in-laws, and friends provided much needed social and emotional support throughout my educational journey.

References

Abelmann, Nancy. 1997. "Narrating Selfhood and Personality in South Korea: Women and Social Mobility." *American Ethnologist* 24, no. 4: 786–812.

Alexander, Karl L., Scott Holupka, and Jack M. Pallas. 1987. "Social Background and Academic Determinants of Two-Year versus Four-Year College." *American Journal of Education* 96, no. 1: 56–80.

Avery, Christopher, and Jonathan D. Levin. 2009. "Early Admissions at Selective Colleges." National Bureau of Economic Research Working Paper Number 14844. http://www.nber.org/papers/w14844.

Ayalon, Hanna, Eric Grodsky, Adam Gamoran, and Abraham Yogev. 2008. "Diversification and Inequality in Higher Education: A Comparison of Israel and the United States." *Sociology of Education* 81, no. 3: 211–241.

Ball, Stephen J., Jackie Davies, Miriam David, and Diane Reay. 2002. "'Classification' and 'Judgement': Social Class and the 'Cognitive Structures' of Choice of Higher Education." *British Journal of Sociology of Education* 23, no. 1:51–72.

Beattie, Irenee R. 2002. "Are All 'Adolescent Econometricians' Created Equal? Racial, Class, and Gender Differences in College Enrollment." *Sociology of Education* 75, no. 1: 19–43.

Benford, Robert D., and David A. Snow. 2000. "Framing Process and Social Movements: An Overview and Assessment." *Annual Review of Sociology* 26:611–639.

Biggart, Andy, and Andy Furlong. 1996. "Educating 'Discouraged Workers': Cultural Diversity in the Upper Secondary School." *British Journal of Sociology of Education* 17(3): 253–266.

Bourdieu, Pierre. 1990. *The Logic of Practice.* Cambridge, UK: Polity Press.

———. 1999. *Language and Symbolic Power.* Cambridge, MA: Harvard University Press.

Bowen, William G., and Derek Bok. 2000. *The Shape of the River: Long-Term Consequences of Considering Race in College and University Admissions.* Princeton, NJ: Princeton University Press.

Bowen, William G., Matthew M. Chingos, and Michael S. McPherson. 2009. *Crossing the Finish Line: Completing College at America's Public Universities.* Princeton, NJ: Princeton University Press.

Bowles, Samuel, and Herbert Gintis. 1976. *Schooling in Capitalist America: Educational Reform and the Contradictions of Economic Life.* New York: Basic Books.

Brand, Jennie E., and Yu Xie. 2010. "Who Benefits Most from College? Evidence for Negative Selection in Heterogeneous Economic Returns to Higher Education." *American Sociological Review* 75, no. 2: 273–302.

Breen, Richard, and John H. Goldthorpe. 1997. "Explaining Educational Differentials: Towards a Formal Rational Action Theory." *Rationality and Society* 9, no. 3: 275–305.

Brewer, Dominic J., Eric R. Eide, and Ronald G. Ehrenberg. 1999. "Does It Pay to Attend an Elite Private College? Cross-Cohort Evidence on the Effects of College Type on Earnings." *Journal of Human Resources* 34, no. 1: 104–123.

Cabrera, Alberto F., Kurt R. Burkum, and Steven La Nasa. 2005. "Pathways to a Four-Year Degree: Determinants of Transfer and Degree Completion among Socioeconomically Disadvantaged Students." In *College Student Retention: A Formula for Student Success*, edited by A. Seidman, 155–209. Westport, CT: Greenwood.

Calarco, Jessica M. 2014. "Coached for the Classroom: Parents' Cultural Transmission and Children's Reproduction of Educational Inequalities. *American Sociological Review* 79, no. 5: 1015–1037.

Carnevale, Anthony P., and Stephen J. Rose. 2004. "Socioeconomic Status, Race/Ethnicity and Selective College Admissions." In *America's Untapped Resource: Low-Income Students in Higher Education*, edited by R. D. Kahlenberg, 101–156. New York: The Century Foundation.

Carter, Prudence L. 2006. "Straddling Boundaries: Identity, Culture, and School." *Sociology of Education* 79, no. 4 : 304–328.

Chin, Tiffani, and Meredith Phillips. 2004. "Social Reproduction and Child-Rearing Practices: Social Class, Children's Agency, and the Summer Activity Gap." *Sociology of Education* 77, no. 3: 185–210.

Desmond, Matthew, and Ruth Lopez Turley. 2009. "The Role of Familism in Explaining the Hispanic-White College Application Gap." *Social Problems* 56, no. 2: 311–334.

Dillon, Eleanor W., and Jeffrey A. Smith. 2013. "The Determinants of Mismatch between Students and Colleges." National Bureau of Economic Research Working Paper Number 19286. http://www.nber.org/papers/w19286.

DiMaggio, Paul. 1997. "Culture and Cognition." *Annual Review of Sociology* 23:263–287.

DiMaggio, Paul J., and Walter W. Powell. 1991. "Introduction." In *The New Institutionalism in Organizational Analysis*, edited by W. W. Powell and P. J. Dimaggio, 1–38. Chicago: University of Chicago Press.

Ewick, Patricia, and Susan Silbey. 2003. "Narrating Social Structure: Stories of Resistance to Legal Authority." *American Journal of Sociology* 108, no. 6: 1328–1372.

Fordham, Signithia, and John U. Ogbu. 1986. "Black Students' School Success: Coping with the Burden of 'Acting White.'" *Urban Review* 18, no. 3: 176–206.

Fuligni, Andrew J., and Sara Pedersen. 2002. "Family Obligation and the Transition to Young Adulthood." *Developmental Psychology* 38, no. 5: 856–868.

Gladieux, Lawrence E. 2004. "Low-Income Students and the Affordability of Higher Education." In *America's Untapped Resource: Low-Income Students in Higher Education*, edited by R. D. Kahlenberg, 17–58. New York: The Century Foundation.

Goffman, Erving. 1974. *Frame Analysis: An Essay on the Organization of the Experience*. Cambridge, MA: Harvard University Press.

Grodsky, Eric, and Catherine Riegle-Crumb. 2010. "Those Who Choose and Those Who Don't: Social Background and College Orientation." *Annals of the American Academy of Political and Social Science* 627, no. 1: 14–35.

Grodsky, Eric, and Erika Jackson. 2009. "Social Stratification in Higher Education." *Teachers College Record* 111, no. 10: 2347–2384.

Grodsky, Eric, and Melanie T. Jones. 2007. "Real and Imagined Barriers to College Entry: Perceptions of Cost." *Social Science Research* 36, no. 2: 745–766.

Hamilton, Laura T. 2016. *Parenting to a Degree: How Family Matters for College Women's Success*. Chicago: University of Chicago Press.

Hamrick, Florence A., and Don Hossler. 1996. "Diverse Information-Gathering Methods in Postsecondary Decision-Making Process." *Review of Higher Education* 19, no. 2: 179–198.

Harding, David J. 2007. "Cultural Context, Sexual Behavior, and Romantic Relationships in Disadvantaged Neighborhoods." *American Sociological Review* 72, no. 3: 341–364.

Hatcher, Richard. 1998. "Class Differentiation in Education: Rational Choices?" *British Journal of Education* 19, no. 1: 5–24.

Hearn, James C. 1991. "Academic and Nonacademic Influences on the College Destinations of 1980 High School Graduates." *Sociology of Education* 64, no. 3: 158–171.

Hill, Catherine B., and Gordon C. Winston. 2006. "How Scarce Are High Ability, Low-Income Students?" In *College Access: Opportunity or Privilege?* edited by M. S. McPherson and M. O. Schapiro, 75–102. New York: College Board.

Horvat, Erin M. 2001. "Understanding Equity and Access in Higher Education: The Potential Contribution of Pierre Bourdieu." In *Higher Education: Handbook of Theory and Research* 16, edited by J. C. Smart and W. G. Tierney, 195–238. New York: Agathon.

Hoxby, Caroline M. 2009. "The Changing Selectivity of American Colleges." *Journal of Economic Perspectives* 23, no. 4: 95–118.

Hoxby, Caroline M., and Christopher Avery. 2012. "The Missing 'One-Offs': The Hidden Supply of High-Achieving, Low-Income Students." National Bureau of Economic Research Working Paper Number 18586. http://www.nber.org/papers /w18586.

Hoxby, Caroline, and Sarah Turner. 2013. "Expanding College Opportunities for High-Achieving, Low Income Students." *Stanford Institute for Economic Policy Research Discussion Paper*, 12, no. 014: 1–42.

Karabel, Jerome, and Alexander W. Astin. 1975. "Social Class, Academic Ability, and College 'Quality.'" *Social Forces* 53, no. 3: 381–398.

Karen, David. 2002. "Changes in Access to Higher Education in the United States: 1980–1992." *Sociology of Education* 75, no. 3: 191–210.

Kelly, Andrew P., and Mark Schneider. 2011. "Filling in the Blanks: How Information Can Affect Choice in Higher Education." American Enterprise Institute for Public Policy Research, 1–36. http://www.aei.org/files/2011/01/12/fillingintheblanks.pdf.

Kim, Jiyun. 2012. "Exploring the Relationship between State Financial Aid Policy and Postsecondary Enrollment Choices: A Focus on Income and Race Differences." *Research in Higher Education* 53, no. 2: 123–151.

Kohn, Melvin L., and Carmi Schooler. 1983. *Work and Personality: An Inquiry into the Impact of Social Stratification*. Norwood, NJ: Ablex.

Lamont, Michele, and Mario L. Small. 2008. "How Culture Matters: Enriching our Understandings of Poverty." In *The Colors of Poverty: Why Racial and Ethnic Disparities Persist*, edited by D. R. Harris and A. C. Lin, 76–102. New York: Russell Sage Foundation.

Lamont, Michele, Stefan Beljean, and Matthew Clair. 2014. "What Is Missing? Cultural Processes and Causal Pathways to Inequality." *Socio-Economic Review* 12, no. 3: 573–608.

Lareau, Annette. 2002. "Invisible Inequality: Social Class and Childrearing in Black Families and White Families." *American Sociological Review* 67, no. 5: 747–776.

Lareau, Annette, and Elliot B. Weininger. 2010. "Class and the Transition to Adulthood." In *Social Class: How Does It Work?*, edited by A. Lareau and D. Conley, 118–151. New York: Russell Sage Foundation.

Lee, Elizabeth M., and Rory Kramer. 2013. "Out with the Old, In with the New? Habitus and Social Mobility at Selective Colleges." *Sociology of Education* 86, no. 1: 18–35.

Lopez Turley, Ruth N., Martin Santos, and Cecilia Ceja. 2007. "Social Origin and College Opportunity Expectations Across Cohorts." *Social Science Research* 36, no. 3: 1200–1218.

MacLeod, Jay. 1987. *Ain't No Makin' It: Aspirations and Attainment in a Low-Income Neighborhood*. San Francisco: Westview Press.

McDonough, Patricia M. 1997. *Choosing Colleges: How Social Class and Schools Structure Opportunity*. New York: State University of New York Press.

McPherson, Michael S., and Morton O. Schapiro. 2006. "Introduction." In *College Access: Opportunity or Privilege?* edited by M. S. McPherson and M. O. Schapiro, 3–15. New York: College Board.

Mickelson, Roslyn A. 1990. "The Attitude-Achievement Paradox among Black Adolescents." *Sociology of Education* 63, no. 1: 44–61.

Morgan, Stephen L. 2005. *On the Edge of Commitment: Educational Attainment and Race in the United States*. Stanford, CA: Stanford University Press.

Mullen, Ann L. 2009. "Elite Destinations: Pathways to Attending an Ivy League University." *British Journal of Sociology of Education* 30, no. 1: 15–27.

———. 2011. *Degrees of Inequality: Culture, Class, and Gender in American Higher Education*. Baltimore, MD: Johns Hopkins University Press

Nash, Roy. 1990. "Bourdieu on Education and Social and Cultural Reproduction." *British Journal of Sociology* 11, no. 4: 431–447.

Ovink, Sarah M., and Demetra Kalogrides. 2015. "No Place like Home? Familism and Latino/a-White Differences in College Pathways." *Social Science Research* 52:219–235.

Perna, Laura W. 2008. "The Role of College Counseling in Shaping College Opportunity: Variations across High Schools." *Review of Higher Education* 31, no. 2: 131–159.

Plank, Stephen B., and Will J. Jordan. 2001. "Effects of Information, Guidance, and Actions on Post-Secondary Destinations: A Study of Talent Loss." *American Educational Research Journal* 38, no. 4: 947–979.

Radford, Alexandria W. 2013. *Top Student, Top School?: How Social Class Shapes Where Valedictorians Go to College*. Chicago: University of Chicago Press.

Roska, Josipa, Eric Grodsky, Richard Arum, and Adam Gamoran. 2007. "United States: Changes in Higher Education and Social Stratification." In *Stratification in Higher Education: A Comparative Study*, edited by Y. Shavi, R. Arum, and A. Gamoran, 165–194. Stanford, CA: Stanford University Press.

Seftor, Neil S., Arif Mamun, and Allen Schirm. 2009. *The Impact of Regular Upward Bound on Postsecondary Outcomes Seven to Nine Years after Scheduled High School Graduation*. Princeton, NJ: Mathematica Policy Research.

Small, Mario L. 2002. "Culture, Cohorts, and Social Organization Theory: Understanding Local Participation in a Latino Housing Project." *American Journal of Sociology* 108, no. 1: 1–54.

Small, Mario L., David J. Harding., and Michele Lamont. 2010. "Reconsidering Culture and Poverty." *ANNALS of the American Academy of Political and Social Science* 629, no. 1: 6–27.

Smith, Jonathan, Matea Pender, and Jessica Howell. 2013. "The Full Extent of Student-College Academic Undermatch." *Economics of Education Review* 32:247–261.

Somers, Margaret R. 1994. "The Narrative Constitution of Identity: A Relational and Network Approach." *Theory and Society* 23, no. 5: 605–649.

Stuber, Jenny M. 2009. "Class, Culture, and Participation in the Collegiate Extra-Curriculum." *Sociological Forum* 24, no. 4: 877–900.

Swail, Watson S., and Laura W. Perna. 2002. "Pre-college Outreach Programs: A National Perspective." In *Increasing Access to College: Extending Possibilities for All Students*, edited by W. G. Tierney and L. S. Hagedorn, 15–34. Albany: State University of New York Press.

Tyson, Karolyn, William Darity Jr., and Domini R. Castellino. 2005. "It's Not 'A Black Thing': Understanding the Burden of Acting White and Other Dilemmas of High Achievement." *American Sociological Review* 70, no. 4: 582–605.

Vaisey, Stephen. 2010. "What People Want: Rethinking Poverty, Culture, and Educational Attainment." *ANNALS of the American Academy of Political and Social Science* 629, no. 1: 75–101.

Villalpando, Octavio, and Daniel G. Solarzano. 2005. "The Role of Culture in College Preparation Programs: A Review of the Research Literature." In *Preparing for College: Nine Elements of Effective Outreach*, edited by W. G. Tierney, Z. B. Corwin, and J. E. Colyar, 13–28. Albany: State University of New York Press.

Webber, Douglas A., and Ronald G. Ehrenberg. 2010. "Do Expenditures Other Than Instructional Expenditures Affect Graduation and Persistence Rates in American Higher Education?" *Economics of Education Review* 29, no. 6: 947–958.

Weiss, Lois, Kristin Cipollone, and Heather Jenkins. 2014. *Class Warfare: Class, Race, and College Admissions in Top-Tier Secondary Schools*. Chicago: University of Chicago Press.

Young, Alford A. 2004. *The Minds of Marginalized Black Men: Making Sense of Mobility, Opportunity, and Future Life Chances*. Princeton, NJ: Princeton University Press.

Zemsky, Robert, and Penney Oedel. 1983. *The Structure of College Choice*. New York: College Board Publications.

Index

academic evaluation rationale, 25–27, 35–36

academic programs: in attendance frameworks, 25–29, 30–31, 32–33, 46; in decision-making frameworks, 15; ethnic resources in availability of, 125; policy implications for, 128; in preparation frameworks, 46, 51–53, 62–63, 67, 68–70; in selection schemas, 22–23, 77–78. *See also* college preparation programs

acceptance letters, 35–36

access: in attendance frameworks, 25; to elite universities, 5–7; to resources and opportunities, 52, 58, 62–65, 67–68, 69–70, 124, 125; in the structure of higher education, 3

adaptation, 53–55, 129

admission: in attendance frameworks, 25–26, 33, 35–36; in preparation frameworks, 49, 68, 69; rates of, 3–4, 18–19; in selection schemas, 76–77, 93, 96; social class in, 120–21, 122

advanced placement (AP) classes, 30–31, 48–49, 50–51, 53, 57, 81, 85

African American students, 13, 21, 31–32, 46–47, 74–75, 95–96, 117, 124–25. *See also* race

afterschool programs, 37, 46. *See also* academic programs

agency: in application choices, 20, 120; in decision-making frameworks, 14; in narratives of interdependence and independence, 23, 99, 110–13, 116–17; in preparation frameworks, 48, 64–65, 69; in selection schemas, 90, 94–95. *See also* autonomy

alternatives. *See* post–high school options

alumni, 82–83, 85–86, 89, 95

any local postsecondary education schema, 74–75

any postsecondary education schema, 20

Asian American students, 21, 27–29, 46–47, 74–75, 95–96, 117, 124–25. *See also* ethnicity; immigrant background; race

assumptions: in attendance frameworks, 21–22, 24–25, 26, 36–44, 45, 46–47, 120–21; in the culture and cognition framework, 14–15; in decision-making frameworks, 7, 8–9, 10; in preparation frameworks, 59. *See also* expectations

attendance frameworks: academic programs in, 25–29, 31–33, 46; anticipation of satisfaction with college in, 25–26, 29–32, 45–46; conscious decision-making in, 21–22, 24–25, 27–28, 36–37, 121; expectations in, 21–22, 24–29, 30–31, 36–44, 45–47, 120–21; moments of certainty in, 24–25, 26–28, 30–33, 35–36, 38–39, 40–41, 42–45, 46–47; multiple options in, 21–22, 24–25, 26–38, 121

autonomy: in narratives of interdependence and independence, 23, 99, 105–6, 110–14,

139

About the Author

YANG VA LOR is an assistant teaching professor in the Department of Sociology at the University of California, Merced.

Available titles in the American Campus series:

Printed and bound by CPI Group (UK) Ltd, Croydon, CR0 4YY

09/06/2025

14685726-0001